Dialogues with the Prophet Mohammed

By

Shahnaaz

ISBN: 1-4140-4832-7 (e-book)
ISBN: 1-4140-4831-9 (Paperback)

Library of Congress Control Number: 2003099701

This book is printed on acid free paper.

Printed in the United States of America
Bloomington, IN

1stBooks – rev. 05/06/04

Preface

I would like to thank my family and Joan and Anne at 1stBooks for their encouragement and constant support that enabled me to write this book.

I feel truly blessed and fortunate to be the chosen one, with the help of my beloved father, the Prophet Mohammed, to have such inspirational dialogues between us.

I hope the reader will be enlightened by the purity of his words in the pages to follow.

Poem

Prophet Mohammed was truly exemplary
His care and concern for all will remain extraordinary

He tried to change a barbaric race
Yet women's oppression and cruelty are still in place

His courage and kindness knew no bounds
His advice always kind, always sound

Throughout history mankind has been full of vanity
Destroying their souls of original purity

He was a great man that would truly care
Injustice, intolerance and cruelty he could not forbear

Like Jesus and Moses before him, he tried in vain
To bring justice to God's name only in pain

In falsehoods his teachings are misconstrued
He only wanted love, humanity and compassion
pursued

I wish he was with us today physically
He has been missed throughout time terribly

Introduction

I am, as my father would say, only a mere mortal. I have no psychic abilities, nor have I ever claimed to be special. What happened to me was not coincidence. It was, I was told, something I had to do for the sake of Islam.

I still question the reason why I was chosen to have these dialogues. Why should I be the privileged one in comparison to thousands of other Moslems? I was no more pious than your average Moslem, nor did I ever do anything particularly exemplarily. It would be a book that would be beneficial not only to the world, but particularly for Islam.

It happened quite unexpectedly. I was sitting at my desk pondering about everything I was told, when all of a sudden I hear "child" in my head. I thought I was hallucinating. Again I hear "child." This time I paid attention and then more words came through until a beautiful conversation ensued.

It has been a wonderful journey ever since and I feel extremely blessed and fortunate to be the chosen one, who is and was able to "channel" my beloved Father. I have, and always will be in awe of him from the moment I had heard that first sound.

The readers, I hope with an open mind, will appreciate his words of total purity. He did not want me to edit his words and I have respected his wishes. I will start with his famous saying to me "remember, Love is all there is."

October 7, 2002

Question: What are your opinions about today's youth?

Answer: The young children, especially the youth of today's society have much to learn and assimilate. Their understanding of humanity, compassion, sharing, caring, kindness and above all of ethics is lacking. The concept of God, religion and morals has diminished. They are living in difficult times, and their struggles to survive in a competitive society are very demanding. Their attitude towards the elders and parents of their societies are one of carelessness.

Their main aim is self directed. There are a few who are totally and sincerely concerned about the older generation. Their opinions of the world around them have to change. Their material attachment toward new and more technological advances are so great that they are drawn to them at any cost. They fail in their concern about their spiritual lives, as their environment and the media only encourage them further.

The company they keep has to be scrutinized, as their influence plays a major role in the shaping of the future outlook and capabilities of the youth.

The bad vices learnt are only going to be a deterrent to them and the future generations to come.

They fail to see the gravity of their behavior onto others. They lack the appreciation of how hard some of their elders and parents have had to work to provide for their current needs.

Question: What do you propose for this generation?

Answer: Understanding, first and foremost, about their future, their attitudes and behavior patterns, and especially how they interact with one another, and as part of society. They have to use their intellect to not only fulfill a current need, but to help benefit themselves 20-25 years from now. They have to take a good look at how hard their parents and grand parents have worked to enable them their current pleasures and resources. How can they benefit themselves, their families and society as a whole? What are their duties as future generations of tomorrow?

Their mannerisms and non tolerant and self-serving attitudes have to change to those of more compassion and humanity. The society and future of the world rest upon them. They can make a difference, most assuredly.

Thank you, Father.

October 8, 2002

Question: Why is there no mention of reincarnation or life after death in the Holy Quran?

Answer: You have to remember, child, it was dictated and written down by many scribes. It was also a time of great turmoil and disturbance amongst the tribes. The people were illiterate and had to have a certain way communicated to them. God has no wrath, but it was written in some cases like that to instill a point. You have to note that there are also metaphors and repetitions done again and again to emphasize. They were people of little education compared to one in today's climate. They were barbaric in nature, and had to have their lessons in a similar but a kind manner told to them for comprehension. I know that a lot of my teachings have been excluded. Realize that reincarnation, most definitely exists, and the Sufi Masters and other Prophets like the Great Buddha, have proven this. Since the time of creation this idea of "karma" has been put in place. The law of nature cannot exist without reincarnation. The Avators like Krishna and Ram attest to it and value the notion very highly. So, yes, daughter, I know that it is not outwardly declared, but it is a very important issue.

3

Shahnaaz

As it was a very difficult concept to grasp for the laymen of that time it was excluded. One has to try and see the situation from the perspective of that time period. I have never been one for rigidity, nor fanaticism at any cost.

Thank you, Father.

Go, child, with the Truth. Bless you.

October 9, 2002

Question: There are so many questions about death and dying. Can you clarify these issues for us?

Answer: Child, all situations vary, each is a special case. Most times it is a quiet passing with the help of our guides and even loved ones. If an individual really wants a particular loved one to come to their aid, then this is the case. Death, you understand, is just a passing into another state, just as coming into birth is a passing of the spirit form into a dense material of a human body, in a mother's womb. The difference being, is that death is in most cases, a return back to our natural state or "home." Life is the school of tests, learning and karma. Destiny, fate and free will are all part of Earth's schooling.

We are basically spirits with experiences we derive from the Earth Plane. Death is our freedom without worries. It is a place of quiet contemplation and wisdom.

Question: Why is there an emotion of fear attached to death?

Answer: Fear is a mental attitude. It is a misconception and a very misunderstood idea. The lack of knowledge of dying gives a person insecurity, which in turn produces fear. It is quite baseless. Actually, what is the fear? Is there a proof that something horrible will be done, or the fact that 'a wrath' will be put onto them? God is mercy, kindness and love. There is no judge or jury. We account for own doings or deeds and we alone are our judge and jury. No one persecutes, or condemns and there is no literal 'hell fire'. How can a spirit with no physical traits "go" to a place of purgatory for their sins when there is no such place? Our guilt is our persecution. We feel what we have done to others. We account for our misdeeds. This is a condemning of a person's own spirit by them. The lack of acceptance in some cases leaves them in "limbo" for a long time before they actually atone for their misgivings.

Question: Michael Newton, a renowned writer of the book "Journey of Souls," has revealed some fascinating information about the Spiritual Realm. Is his research factual?

Answer: His research, into what you would call the "paranormal" is quite accurate. He is indeed one of a few who has done a remarkable job in really focusing on the spiritual realm. He deals with different levels of soul development, as well as their journey, both to and from Earth as well. I would say, child, the closest study of the other side.

Question: So his book could be used as reference material about life after death?

Answer: Yes, in many ways. It is always wise to acquire knowledge as it takes away the fear of the unknown. Michael is an evolved soul, whose journey is to help others in this lifetime. He is a very good example of this. Mankind has much to learn.

Many evolved souls come to the Earth plane to be a teacher or to invoke the Truth. Their methods vary, but their goal or purpose is essentially the same.

His book is quite factual and written with much honesty. Remember each soul comes to the Earth plane for a purpose. There is so much confusion and misconception about death, dying and life after death that these types of books are extremely useful.

Question: What do you think of Regression Therapy?

Answer: Each past life has its own merit on the soul and its existence. Relying or questioning one's past lives serves no real purpose. God made us forget so that we can accomplish our current lifetime without dwelling in the past. Regression is good for a cure purpose. That is, if there is a physical ailment with no medical cure. However, remember that it is also harmful. Sometimes, whilst finding solutions, we tend to dwell in a past life situation. This can deter our present growth or affect us currently. If it brings a form of complete closure on a particular problem, then it is helpful. I firmly believe in finding solutions primarily in the present. I am not trying to deter past life regression therapy, but this should be a last case scenario. Realize we are components of many lives and the various developments. Our soul comprises many series of events and learning experiences. This is soul growth, learning and development.

Thank you, Father, for your insights.

Child, life is a learning process. The intellect is a tool to be used for the benefit of oneself, one's family and one's society. It should be used for the betterment of all, not for the destruction or creation of injustice, lies and propaganda. God wants us to use our intellect consciously and for love. It is indeed a powerful tool not to be misused to bring about harm in anyway or gain on

7

another's expense. The intellect is a blessing from God for the betterment of society.

Child, go with love, peace and understanding.

October 10, 2002

Question: What is the meaning of the word Karma, and how is it connected to one's destiny?

Answer: Karma, child, is what you have brought from your past incarnations, and what you create on an on going basis. Based on this, an individual's destiny is preordained. However, man is also master of his/her destiny and of their future. That is, despite a person's karma, he can make changes to his current life to improve and change some parts of his destiny.

Question: Can you elaborate and give an example, please?

Answer: Yes, child, I can. For example, a child who is born in poverty has to learn certain life lessons in his current incarnation. The life lessons would be to appreciate hunger, suffering and forbearance that he lacked in his prior incarnation. If he understands that his current situation is hopeless, and that he cannot change it in anyway, then his destiny is maintained. However, if he earnestly, with faith in himself and in God, tries to make a difference so that both he and his family can have a better life, rest assured, God will come to his aid. Someone, might for example,

9

out of mercy, decide on looking at his family's plight and give them some financial aid. The family in turn will then try enabling this child to obtain some sort of education.

He will work hard and go to places of higher learning, like a university, and excel himself to succeed. His success will then lead to his financial stability, which in turn will aid his family as well. This poverty stricken family is now in a better financial standing than it was originally.

Question: This sounds like a 'ripple' or domino effect?

Answer: Yes, exactly. It all depends on a person's outlook. Determination, intent and above all faith in God is very important. Child, the underlying question is how hard is the person's intent and how strong their faith in God? It is very important on how much, or how far one wants to achieve success. Often, despite our hopes and aspirations, we may lack faith in God and even in ourselves. God, in his mercy, always sends aid in different ways. Their conviction in his mercy only obligates God, our Father, to bring his kindness onto them.

God, child, sees, hears, understands and feels all. A child with complete faith, for example, in God, is helped at all times. God, in his infinite mercy, is always there to open doors that were closed before for all who seek his help. This is a very important issue and has to be addressed.

Question: Father, can we discuss relationships? Does karma dictate whether they are to remain single or unattached?

Answer: Again, child, their preordained karma comes into play. Many times, an individual is not capable of sustaining a relationship due to his character or attitude, and in this case, it is better that he or she remains unattached.

Other times, they are lucky enough to have karma with long term partners to not only procreate for future generations, but also to help in their partners sustenance. They also gain in this bond in other areas as well. Relationships, as explained before, are based on past life karma. That is, if we have ties and links with different individuals on various levels, and we have not completed 'our path' with them in prior incarnations, we have to 'come back' and resolve our issues with them, and definitely be a part of their lives when we incarnate once again.

Question: Can you give us an example?

Answer: Let us take a woman who was badly mistreated by her husband in a prior lifetime. The husband, will in this lifetime have the onus to resolve many issues with her. A lot of times, the lesson is learnt through role reversal. He will now understand and feel what it is like to be the wife. It is very important to forgive one another so that we have no attachments that need to be resolved in future lifetimes.

Question: Are children also part of the law of karma?

Answer: Most certainly. Souls that have not finished their ties to other individuals can come as children. It all depends on their past connections with other souls. Mankind is controller of their destiny in choosing whom they would like to be with and in what capacity. Often, we will want our children because we chose them before incarnating onto the Earth plane. Michael's book is very descriptive of the many types of soul births, and especially of group souls.

Each soul before incarnating, has to try and resolve their issues of their past life incarnations with others. Again to forgive all those that harm or are indebted to us is very crucial. When we

11

forgive, we are in essence cleaning out our past karma and linkages, and we do not need to incarnate with those individuals. It is always better not to come back to a world that will only lead one to be materialistic and Earthbound.

The Karmic Wheel of Life can cease if one can comprehend that most people are ignorant. That is, if they truly knew that hurting or harming another would be and is detrimental to their soul, would they continue to be a certain way? Evil doers have to pay a heavy price for their wrong doings. A person's good and bad karma carries over with them in future incarnations. This enables one to be successful or unhappy. Their current behavior is a setting for future incarnations. For example, if a successful employer mistreats his employees, he will have to account and resolve for his misdeeds by coming back with them in a future incarnation.

In the same manner, if a person, due to his past good karma, incarnates, he will benefit in his current lifetime.

He obviously has to maintain his deeds or he will be unsuccessful the next time he incarnates. It is a continuous phenomenon. Why destroy oneself? What was and is the point? Why not stop the reincarnation process?

Will mankind ever realize that greed, temptation, material pleasure and vices surely draw an individual into painful future incarnations? Our deeds always account for each incarnation. No one is exempt, child. Nothing is coincidence and everything is always done for a reason. Our so called 'chance meetings' are not that at all. They were preordained. Again Michael Newton's books give one a better perception of soul birth and rebirth.

Thank you, Father.

October 11, 2002

Question: Can you help define what depression is and how to overcome it?

Answer: Depression is a very legitimate state of mind. Mankind has to understand that life is a fragment of a time span compared to the one in the Spiritual Realm. We get so accustomed to the material world that we allow it to draw on our faculties.

Mankind forgets that life here is temporal. Our interactions, life style and existence are not permanent. We dwell in our current existence as if it will last forever. We allow our surroundings to affect us in our life span and get "depressed" because of it. If we were to comprehend and realize that it was unimportant and that our pain and affliction were only Earthbound with no real substance or meaning, merely learning lessons, we would not lose hope, feel despair or be despondent.

Understanding where the emotions stem from is important. Is it worthwhile and beneficial, daughter? Or is it detrimental enough to impact on our well being? Everything in life has to be taken in perspective. Was the thought worth it?

Daughter, if we take on all that we go through personally, not understanding that there are lessons to be learnt, then it would

13

affect us. Lessons or tests only help spiritually cleanse, which mankind cannot understand or relate to. They are so immersed in their day to day chores to know why they are suffering.

Faith and trust are very big issues. We have to believe in God and know that regardless of our lessons in life, he will assist us in any situation. Our prayers are never unheard. With true faith he always delivers. His angels are always ready to help and his compassion knows no bounds. It may take time, but it does indeed come. Everything is done for a reason. Nothing is invalid. Prayers do move mountains. One's faith is very important. Sometimes, what we want is not what is essential for us and we do not see the reasons at the time.

Thank you, Father. That was very beneficial.

Bless you, child, go in peace and enlightenment.

October 12, 2002

Question: What are your views on organized religion?

Answer: Religion, child, is for most people, a form of worship brought down from their ancestral beliefs and cultures. Depending on a society's past belief, they will instill these views on their children and their future generations. Whether organized or not, if done for one's benefit, without harming another within their society or outside of their culture, it is also beneficial. Religion, in a sense, brings about discipline and helps them become more of a focused race. It also helps bring about groups of individuals in one united effort to better themselves and those around them. Religion, is and was, a part of a learning process, and an understanding that we are but a small part of an overall creation. A learning process that enables a person to understand that our sustenance on a daily basis is not due to us, but due to a Divine Essence, who watches us and loves us despite our misgivings. If the current society today, through their organized religions, brought about by the teachings of the Prophets, enabled individuals to learn not just the appreciation of their current lives, but to understand the concept of their souls, then this would be very beneficial. Religion, if used for the benefit of the Elders, Priests or Gurus alone is completely wrong and baseless. This type of 'religion' is detrimental to that society that follows their tenements.

Question: Does a person have to be religious to be worthy in God's eyes?

Answer: The belief in God is beneficial, as he alone provides for all beings. However, if a nonbeliever does not believe and is skeptic and harmless to both society and his family, he is considered in God's eyes also worthy. All are God's children despite their various points of view. In fact, child, being a humane nonbeliever, is in God's eyes, better than a believer who is self serving and harmful to others.

A person who proclaims to be a believer and is a terrorist, who uses religion to front his cause, is not only a hypocrite, but is condemned by God. Kind, compassionate and understanding individuals are better than hypocrites. They are totally looked down upon and disregarded. They are a total disgrace upon society. What is their gain here and in the hereafter? Individuals fail to look at their actions especially for the future of their souls.

Question: What makes Islam a better religion in comparison to others?

Answer: No one religion is better than the other. All religions, whether it is Judaism, Christianity or Islam taught the concept of God and humanity. All religions came into place at different times depending on the need of that particular era. When the human race has reached a point of barbarism, inhumanity and cruelty, God, in his mercy, sends upon them his Prophets to change their ways. Islam was the last religion to take root in this world. It was a religion that came into being onto a barbaric and illiterate race. This race of people happened to be cruel individuals from the East and were of Arab descent.

Question: What is the underlying thread in all three of the world's religions?

Answer: Monotheism, humanity, kindness, love amongst each other and total submissiveness to God.

Thank you, Father.

Child, many times many questions arise in one's mind. We have to address them and put them in proper perspective.

Go with love, compassion and understanding.

October 13, 2002

Question: What, Father, in your opinion, would be the perfect type of government in any country or state?

Answer: *A government that truly hears the plight of their people, whose concern is for, of and to the people like the type Plato had advocated in his writings. Understand, that many governments advocate these views externally, but they are totally self centered and corrupt in nature. They are a government with self serving and ego bound individuals. Instead of helping their country, they help themselves only. Their underlying motive is to get elected and they will proclaim and promise whatever the masses want to hear. However, their intentions are anything but honorable.*
There are also politicians in power, who bring about governments that ultimately are a destruction to their people. A government leader and individuals within that government body have to look at the country, the people, the environment and its neighboring countries before they can make sound decisions.
Their country and its components not only play a major role in their people's lives, but also to the environment they live in and to the neighboring countries around them. A good gov-

ernment would bring about pluralism, good health and benefit packages, education and social welfare for the people. They would take the people's point of view on all issues before making decisions. No law or jurisdiction would be set up without compliance from their people. Their policies would bring about equality of sexes, creed and color. Their environment policies would take into account Earth's Eco System which would help in mankind's future environment.

A government, child, where consideration of the smallest or largest issue would be tackled with understanding of all human needs. This is very vital for a good government to be in place in any country or state.

Thank you, Father.

Go in peace, child.

October 14, 2002

Question: We live in a material world full of self-centered, "me-first" people. Do you think we will continue to be satisfied with such self-serving thinking?

Answer: For a while this will continue until after a century when the soul will be awakened into spiritual awareness. People will then realize that there is more to life, then their bodies and their material comforts. That life has to have more meaning than their current existence. The question of where did it begin and when will be the end will be utmost in most minds and thought processes.

Question: There are so much negativity, angst, anger, hurt, betrayal, and killing in this world. Why so much turmoil? We have no security, and we live in fear.

Answer: When there is no self satisfaction and everyone wants a better material world, where there is no respect, greed is insurmountable and the ego holds up despite any consequences, the result will be a travesty. Mankind has to understand that we are all ultimately the same energy as God. All of God's children are created equally. The strife and unrest are only due to their ignorance and mistrust amongst themselves.

Question: How do you account for brutal killing, abductions, stealing and other prevalent and horrifying acts?

Answer: Childhood abuse, dissatisfaction, ego and tormented minds are the result of such actions. Love is the solution, care for each other, humanity and brotherhood. Parental responsibility is the sole cause. Parents forget their duties. They bring into this world future generations that effect society as a whole. The environment, media and society only contribute to the end result.

I feel so honored and blessed that you have allowed me to be able to telepathically communicate with you. Thank you. I am truly in awe. Each time I talk to you I have a feeling of peace, serenity and security. Always comforting and always there to help me.

Child, for many years you have been seeking answers to many questions. You have asked questions for the knowledge of life, truth, creation and above all suffering. You have been tormented by these issues and tormented also both spiritually and materially. Your quest for knowledge gave you much wisdom. Much knowledge was advanced to you and you learned a lot. There are still many questions as to various unanswerable issues and conflicts in your mind.

You are a defender of the truth. You are a Sufi in all aspects. You still have much to learn and understand.

The mental and emotional suffering you have gone through has brought you much anguish and sorrow. Your distress has also cleansed your soul. Your life lessons have been learned and you need not worry about anguish anymore.

Shahnaaz

Trials and tribulations, although being life's journey, don't have to damage one's emotional being to the point of destruction. You have prayed earnestly and wanted and sought much.
Direct communication was the best way to help you fulfill your quests. Also, it is through you, many will learn, assimilate and understand God and life.

Thank you, Father.

Bless you child, go in peace.

November 4, 2002

Question: Father, what is the true meaning of the word Sufism?

Answer: Sufism is piety at its best. It is compassion and love without condition. It is brotherhood done selflessly. It is the search for the Truth in all aspects of one's life. It is like a new day where every minute is contemplated for the good of one and for mankind. Sufism understands the quest of life and how to help others understand the right and true path. It is being able to adhere to the principles of virtue and respect to all creatures. It is without ego, pride and vanity. The search for true love and of the reaching into oneness is its beauty.

A true Sufi will never proclaim themselves, but their actions and words will bring forth their essence. They are ascetics without giving up their lives and suffering in physical turmoil. They can balance the material and the spiritual and still remain in the Truth. A true Sufi does not need a cave, an Ashram or a mountaintop. They do not have to follow strict rules and regiments and suffer. The way they conduct their lives and their attitudes and intents to all around them are their Truth. They are examples of what mankind should be. Their way of life is teaching enough to others around them. From their behavior derives an individual of fortitude and tolerance. Silence is their greatest virtue and they carry this with great honor.

Question: We see many people leaving their material lives and going to live in Ashrams as ascetics. Is this necessary for the improvement of one's soul?

Answer: That is not necessary. Each individual came with a purpose into their lives with their destiny preordained. By not completing this, they have to come again to fulfill their various links and connections with others. Religion, devotion, Sufism or the quest to "oneness" is not a force, nor did God want to impose any form of turmoil or pain in achieving this status. Living a life like a Sufi is all he desires of his children.

Question: So, in other words, we can enjoy the benefits of a material life and at the same time be spiritual?

Answer: Yes, correct. That is the true mode of living. ***Again I emphasize*** *that* ***no extra concern to one over the other is needed****. It should be a balanced lifestyle. The material world should not put one in a compromising situation nor should one be totally spiritual. Our duties to society, family and our surroundings are fundamental.*

Thank you, Father.

Go with blessings and peace child. God is ever present and ever loving

November 5, 2002

Question: Father, there are many Ashrams being created around the world. Can you explain the concept of being a 'Guru'?

Answer: Child, a Guru, is a leader with his own method of teachings. Like a Master, a true Guru is well versed in what he reveals and teaches. There are many falsehoods about some Gurus. The need comes about for a Guru when there is a search for knowledge. Most times it is necessitated out of a yearning to know more about the complexities of life. A true Master has no ego, he has no need for a financial reward, nor charges fees for his services, unless the devotee needs to learn for the benefit of himself, and the Master is not able to sustain his present worldly condition. A true Guru's main goal is to benefit his followers with his teachings that he himself has mastered from his own practices over the years. He is coming from purity, where there is no ego or pride in his lessons. His goal is not of self recognition or grandiosity, but of helping another in spiritual matters. He is someone who knows and has the best interests of his pupils at heart. His only aim is basic sustenance and teachings for the benefit of others.

Question: There are psychics, mediums, fortune-tellers, palmists and clairvoyants. What are your opinions regarding them?

Answer: Child, the power of the 6th sense does exist. Some with increased soul awareness either from their past lives, or through pure meditation, they have been given these blessings. There are various stages to one's gifts. Each individual has his/her capacity of foresight. However, not everyone claiming to have increased foresight is honest. There are many that are only partially sensory and capitalize on this. This can be seen in the palmist and tarot readers. These are a learned art. They are not true psychics or clairvoyants and not mediums at all.

Question: Some of these psychics abuse their power and take advantage of people's monetary resources.

Answer: Yes, that is very true. Understand, child, when it is not for the betterment of an individual, and also to show one the truth in helping become more spiritual, it is abuse. Just knowing a future is not enough. There has to be some form or benefit derived from the reading. When a reading is done, it should not only help resolve a problem, but help the individual understand why the problem is there in the first place.

How does it relate to them from their past lives? How does the problem affect them mentally, spiritually and on a physical level?

A good example, would be to take a person tormented in pain, who is seeking an answer to their situation. Going to the root of the problem, with "hands on healing" is one way.

Also, they have to help that person understand and see what the person's mental attitude is at that particular point in time.

This method is very effective in bringing about a resolution of the problem. Just showing one their future, without really helping the present situation, is not a true reading. How can the person overcome today's problems, with more awareness, is very essential.

Question: Would you be able to give us an example?

Answer: If an individual, for example, wants to know about future companionship, the psychic should try and help their current situation first, and then determine if they can see the predestined event. If there is no companionship, then they can help them understand the reasoning behind it. Is that individual happy at present? What happened in their previous past lives, their current past life, and if there is a future relationship how to manage it and think it through. Our attitudes allow our lives to carry a course negatively or positively. We are the roads to our destiny. How badly do we seek something and how much do we believe in it to establish it in the future? Our destiny can also make us desire something different as well. Are we masters of our destiny? Yes, absolutely. But, realize also that wanting, hoping and expecting within realistic bounds are essential. We cannot wish or expect something unrealistic or undeserving. Was it meant? The healing of the present is very important as well. It will give one the strength to understand why we can or cannot achieve our goals.

Question: If a person sought wealth for their future happiness, would this be considered unrealistic?

Answer: What would they desire it for, and for what benefit? A true psychic would first know and see the reason, and then with that person's past life knowledge at hand, determine if this is their karma or not. A good medium would not only help a person understand their reason for their lack of not being wealthy, but also how to be more spiritually inclined. Advice on how to better their lives to enable their wishes to take fruit would be a good solution.

Question: So a good psychic has a heavy burden imposed on them?

Answer: Yes, and no child. What is the motive behind the psychic? Just monetary or do they want to help you understand the root of your problem. Allowing you to ask for solutions and aiding you in all your efforts for a better future environment is very essential. This can be done in any given area.

Question: There are a lot of skepticism and disbeliefs about psychics.

Answer: Skepticism is a real emotion and should not be mocked. Honoring what is true is important. There are many false pretenders and liars. Faith in God is supreme, but if one feels the need to go to a psychic, a proper test of that psychic is needed. What method and how are they going to help you is vital.

Again one's faith in God is above all else, but sometimes we need a form of encouragement or motivation. Palmistry and Tarot cards are temporal aids and not necessarily a future benefit. As days, attitudes and situations do change, so does one's fate. Our thoughts are powerful tools and can co-create a lot in our lives. The concept of positive thinking is very crucial. Hope is vital in all areas.

Each day is a blessing. Faith in God is essential and our attitude is again important. We are all on a journey, preordained and predestined, but most importantly with a free will. We alone can follow, accept, improve or damage our destiny.

Question: Can you explain the concept of synchronicity?

Answer: Well, if we are traveling, for example, and we are destined to meet our future partner, and we do indeed meet them, and they seem nice and all that we desire, we might feel that they are all we have been searching for. However, up until that point, we have had a very insecure and negative life. Will we really want or believe we can have or want this situation?

We may have doubts about the situation or think we are going to lose it and don't give it a chance, or put on an attitude to damage the situation to bring it to a halt. What then of a preordained fate? Our free will comes into play here. Allowing it to continue is advisable, but not if it is determined to hurt or damage us. In other words, take a chance and see how it feels, how does it really make us truly feel?

Do we feel respect, love, cherished and secure? All decisions have free will; there cannot be force by external pressures. God didn't give mankind free will to be oppressed by another's will.

Oppression, suppression and any kind of abuse are wrong and not part of humanity. No one, whoever they are, is allowed to treat another into a situation of their dislike. No one should be mistreated or harmed in any way. Any form of abuse to another is totally unacceptable. It not only affects the other, but it demoralizes them and also harms them spiritually. All of us good or bad are God's children. Why not come to terms with each other? Why not help each other? Standing up for oneself, is only showing respect to oneself which is God's creation. Each one of us is beautiful in our own way. Each one of us is on a destiny of his/her own.

When a soul hurts or harms another he is hurting or harming himself.

Of what gain was the action? Life, child, is a blink of an eye to eternity.

Death is never far and our actions and deeds are all we carry and take with us. No material baggage should encumber us or burden us in the spiritual world. Listen, understand, watch, look and above all learn. Only our own intellect, with proper understanding and wisdom, is the solution.

That was magnificent and truly inspirational, Father, thank you.

Child, life has much to look forward to and much to understand. Each day is a lesson. Through every person's pain and sorrow, and through every person's happiness is a lesson as well. Take with each moment its blessings and remain in peace.

Love, is all there is, and total and complete trust in God is essential. Make no unnecessary compromises in any painful situation, but bring about solutions. Discussions and intellectual understanding are the key solutions in any given arena.

Thank you again.

Bless you child and go in peace, love and knowledge.

November 6, 2002

Question: Father, can you tell me about the benefits of prayer?

Answer: First of all, prayer gives a person complete humility, as we understand and realize that there is above us a Divine Source. This Divine Source, or God, is what maintains all beings and protects and nurtures each of us. When an individual prays, he is submitting himself/herself to Allah, the Most Merciful.

Each religion or Moslem sect, such as the Shias and Sunnis prostrate themselves regularly to Allah. It is only through prayer that we have the "faith" that Allah will give us sustenance and uplift our spiritual beings. Each and every one of us as I have said is a "spark" of this Divine Source. Each time we pray, we illuminate this spark. When we meditate, we are trying to have our soul connect to this Source or Divine Spirit. It is only through our daily behavior, or realization of our behavior, that we attain self-consciousness. This encompasses respect, concern, brotherhood, compassion and understanding toward each another. When we, with our self-consciousness, meditate on a regular basis, we are able to connect to Allah.

This constant connection and our constant realization of our behavior, then helps us get to Fana Fillah or Nirvana as the great Buddha put it. There is no distinction between God and all of man's surroundings. Every atom and/or molecule in the universe and beyond is part of Allah or the Divine Spirit. Thus, to achieve this 'state of perfection', one has to be balanced on a material and a spiritual level.

Prayer is food for the soul if said alone, but child, with or in a congregation it is highly intensified. When prayers are done with many others at the same time, the effect is tenfold. Each prayer is like a beautiful beam reaching God. When there are many "beams" together, the effect is magnified and illuminating. It enhances the experience, most assuredly, child.

Question: Father, Edgar Cayce, the famous psychic, used to say that there are "Many Mansions" in the spiritual realm? Also do you feel that the Michael Newton's book "Journey of Souls" gives us a true portrayal of what the spiritual realm is all about?

Answer: Yes, there are many or seven realms in the Spiritual World. The higher a person's spiritual growth attained on the Earth Plane through their deeds and prayer, the higher the ascension for them in the spiritual realm. Each soul's deeds determine which level or "sphere" is the seat of that soul after their demise. Therefore, it is very wise to understand or have this perception when living here on the Earth plane. The lower realms are not a place any child should dwell in, in the hereafter.

There are many books on the spiritual realm, but I feel that the best ones are written by Michael Newton.

When one does meditate, many answers to questions sought are given to the seeker, once they attain a higher spiritual state. The Earth plane is temporal, and a mortal's life is limited. Keeping this in mind, one can only understand the intensity of how one's behavior determines their spiritual existence.

That was phenomenal, Father, thank you.

Child, understanding the fundamentals of existence here and in the spiritual realm is very crucial to every mortal. The 'Karmic Wheel of Life', is also important to understand. The eastern religious concept of our destiny and karma is very significant. The avatars like Ram and Krishna explained or detailed this perfectly. Each of us has to understand the esoteric and exoteric concepts of life. Mankind cannot live only for material betterment, and feel that there is a void after death. We all have the Divine Spark, and we all, like little drops of a river, have to return to our Father, the big and vast ocean. Annihilation is the key word for the soul. I pray, that each individual understands the gravity of this discussion.

It is the intent that counts. Prayer for the benefit of others does count. When parents pray, they are doing a duty for the improvement of their child. God loves humanity and anything done for humanity's sake counts. It is prayer for another soul, another universal being.

Question: Is there a ritual to prayers?

Answer: Daughter, prayer is prayer. There is no better prayer or stronger one. All are names of God. One can take out one prayer with love, feeling and intent and it is the same as saying 1000. Quality not quantity is essential.

Question: Many Moslems do ritualistic prayers. Can you comment on this?

Answer: Suffering for the benefit of others is beneficial, but need not harm oneself. If they feel their prayers will be answered and the inner feeling is so strong, they can do this. Remember

God hears at all times and is ever present. He listens even for a second if it is a prayer from the heart. Purity, faith, understanding and love are the critical elements here. The duration is up to each individual. Love and faith determine the outcome. If prayers are said for self gratification, harm or self interest, it is baseless.

Question: Different perspective, Father, what is the issue about homosexuality? How does God regard this?

Answer: God does not judge or make judgement. Each life is lead by each individual. He does not dislike anyone. We are his creations, his children.

Question: But there is no mention in the Holy Quran about them?

Answer: It was not public then, nor were they allowed as you say to "come out." Society and its many rules dictate how mankind should live and behave.

Question: Is it preordained that they should live a life in this situation?

Answer: Yes, they chose to be like this. The ridicule by society is a learning lesson from past lives. Their partners have agreed to be with them in this lifetime.

Question: So it was preordained?

Answer: Absolutely. Sometimes an individual is not happy in their "skin"; they change, as their lives are not fruitful. This is not karma. This is intentional. Each situation is different. God does not judge. His concern is love and humanity.

Question: What about the Mormons who have say 8-9 wives and live in a sort of communion? Is this the destiny for their wives?

Answer: Yes and no. The cycle of karma is there. We meet and we can make lives together or we can change our decisions.

Question: What of the children of these relationships?

Answer: Each soul has the right to come into various surroundings. This is their karma. If a soul does not want to love, come into creation or procreate, it is their free will.

Question: Is it not a sin to have so many wives?

Answer: Sin is a word associated with man. Wrong doing to be more precise if any one of these wives suffers or is treated unequally. No one can totally and completely treat another with total equality. Everything has to be seen in a proper perspective.

Thank you, Father for your wisdom.

Bless you child, go with peace, harmony and wisdom.

The material world is hard to comprehend, daughter, but we have to adhere and be patient. God, bless you.

November 8, 2002

Question: Can you explain the concept of the Burkha or Hijab, which is the covering for women in Islam?

Answer: Daughter, initially, before my "Nabuwat," society had transgressed terribly. There was no shame, no decency and no respect. Women were treated as chattels. Anyone could possess any woman. They had no say, no rights and no form of speech. Oppression was abound and so was suppression. Every egoistic male dominated the society that governed all decisions. No woman felt safe or content or had any self-esteem. They were treated badly and like belongings or like the animal's one owned. It was a turbulent time. It was a time of absolute discourse and distrust.

Since my childhood, I could not fathom any creature, let alone a human being suffering such wrath. It was terrible to see, to witness and to listen to the down trodden 'woman'.

What of their plight? Were they not human beings like the men? Did they not feel, and want to be respected? Were these women not their mothers and sisters? Did they not cater to their needs? They were human beings that needed to voice their equality, their intelligence and be in equal standing alongside the men. They had the same if not more tolerance, persistence and understanding to life than the men. Their substance was even better and they could outdo a man anytime. I watched only helplessly and in suffering and in a quiet rage. Was there no justice to this infliction and was there no end to this cruelty? I persevered until I received my duty to the call of God or my Nabuwat.

Question: Bibi Khadija, your wife, was older than you. Did you have to undergo much frustration and tension because of this in that archaic society?

Answer: Child, I respected and acknowledged how not only kind, generous, astute and understanding she was, but how much wisdom she had as well. Beauty was her inner essence. She was amazing. I was literally in awe. The age issue never was a question. Khadija was so pure of character that it never occurred to me to look at her from a worldly perspective. She was a gift, a Godsend in every way. Our love was pure, without condition and without a lack of want in anything.

I was not bothered about society and its misgivings, or about the rules and regulations. Why would I want to follow such abhorrent people's confirmation? Why would I want their approval? I always felt that man had a special place in life and that nothing was coincidence. This I knew intrinsically. My soul knew that there was more to life than just mere living. My going to Mt. Hira for solitude for hours on end was to find the answers to these questions. A creator who made this creation had to have a reason for all that was going on.

Question: How did you feel when Gabriel came upon you?

Answer: My Nabuwat not only dazzled and stunned me, but I was in deep awe, almost like a spiritual shock. I had a very strong disbelief and a fear of the unknown after this experience. Was this really happening to me? Why me? Oh my God, literally. Gabriel was beautiful, supporting, loving, kind and inspiring. He is one of God's greatest Angels and a gift to mankind. An extremely evolved Angel, Gabriel is so loving that one cannot imagine how much he can care.

Question: Can you still clarify the issue of the Hijab?

Answer: Yes, the Hijab. Well, indecent exposure only brings about an encouragement to the wayward eye. Lust was very rampant. It was so strong and its consequences that it was totally shameful. My aim was to curtail this attitude. I tried to bring about respect for that time period, and to have women looked upon as individuals, and not objects of desire or of satisfying one's needs.

Question: The full covering still continues today in most Moslem countries. Do you feel this is necessary?

Answer: Daughter, as times change, so should the attitude. No, it is not necessary for the women to wear this Hijab. We live in an educated globe, where technology knows no bounds, and yet we adhere to disrespect women. Why? If women are dressed conservatively, they do not have to have a Hijab. Society knows its boundaries and its limits. Education and the intellect know how one can dictate one's life. Do you think women today would allow subjugation, abuse and harassment?
 The world has changed and people have to change their mentalities. The Umma has to forego their control issues and submit to the realities of the changing times. Brotherhood, love and hu-

manity are what I taught. When we continue with our modes of thought we are agreeing to go against the principles I strongly believed in and adhered to.

I look at the world over time and feel really sad at the state of how women are still being treated unfairly. The world has to have peace and tranquility, where no race controls or harms, and where no one country is superior over another. There is so much torment and materialistic subjugation in the minds of people that it brings about outrageous acts onto a person. What is this for? What necessitates one human being to loathe another? Are we not all God's creation? How can one person be more superior to another? Were we not all created equally? Where is it shown that a black, brown or white man has different blood or organs? The skin is different, as God placed his different children in different climatic conditions on Earth. Does this mean we resort to racism? Hate? Dislike to the point of killing?

Question: Father, you sound upset?

Answer: Yes, child, very unhappy. God's children are suffering. Pain in any form is still pain. It pains me to see these wrong doings happening every minute on Earth. How did my teachings get so that they are being used in falsehood? The egos of superiors of countries and the disturbed minds of Moslem fanatics claim they are doing this in the name of religion? God, from whom religion comes from, in any religion, forbade killing outright in any form or manner. Why then do we take his name in vain? Why do we transgress so?
Why do they not heed to the Truth?

Question: What do you propose Father?

Shahnaaz

Answer: Intellectual decision-making, unity of minds, mutual humanistic understanding by one global movement. If we all stood as God's creatures, side by side, fought for the Truth, the situation would improve. Groups should continue to speak up, take action, and this should happen from the educated masses. The leaders have to listen to the educated masses of today. They don't want pain, infliction and suffering. It is then and only then that the world would be a better place to live in for our children and the future generations and for us. Does not humanity surpass all issues of the ego? There has to be one global thinking to necessitate big changes on Earth. Many groups or reformists are coming up as there is too much unrest. Is a bloodshed worth it? How much pain is going to take place globally through the evil doers or terrorists before the world leaders listen?

Thank you, Father for the profound and insightful statements.

Thank you, child, for your time and patience. Go with peace, blessings and wisdom. Love is all there is.

November 9, 2002

Question: Father, I think I understand the covering of one's body, but is the face covering necessary?

Answer: In those days daughter, even a pretty face caused much disruption. Hence the complete coverage was necessary. There are many revolts taking place at present to remove the Burkha and Hijab and persecution is still inevitable. It has and still is, unfortunately, a very male dominated society. The Taliban was a very horrible example of this male domination. For centuries women have been treated very unjustly. The Mullahs and Moslem policemen in association with the authorities have always enforced this rigid regiment. The only way the women, my children, can overcome this oppression is by using a group force. I mean really protesting with the educated women to fight this unfair attitude. They should stand up vocally, even though it is difficult, and view their ideas. It is very difficult, I understand, for the uneducated women in small towns and countries, where the fear of being punished is rampant.

Question: You taught that both men and women were equal

41

as far as intelligence was concerned.

Answer: Very much the issue. I not only preached this, but tried to put it to practice especially amongst my wives and my daughters, including Fatima. No woman felt intimidated or a lesser being at that time at all. All people are God's creatures and equal in intellect and feeling. I totally abhorred slavery and feel that it is coming back again. When a man mistreats his wife, this is truly shameful. What they don't understand is that a woman is just as smart or even more reliable than a man. Look how much they do. They are mothers, teachers, sisters and wives. They are partners in all walks of life. There are no professions currently that a woman cannot do. Their fortitude and emotional understanding far outweigh that of any man. In fact, if a woman had ruled a country without any ego or greed, she would far surpass its improvement than a man ruler could. Their emotional well being and maternal instincts would put into place better facilities for all. It would be a very liberated and democratic state that also had boundaries for safety. The ego for power, if properly governed, would not be there. It would be a state, like Plato advocated, "for the people and of the people." It is only through the mother that children can learn mannerisms, respect, behavior, attitude, belief, concern and humanity. Women are terribly underrated and even in the Western world highly underpaid. This is truly sad.

Question: Do you think this trend will become less over the years?

Answer: Hopefully, with more intellectual and educated children, it should improve. Women realize this wrongdoing and in their own efforts are trying very hard to overcome this facet of control. My desire, daughter, is for world awareness. I want for the children of every race to understand women, and also for women to understand their roles in society. They play a very significant role. They shape the future generations through an example and also through their speech.

Thank you, Father, that was truly enlightening.

Bless you child, go in peace and love.

November 10, 2002

Question: Can we discuss certain notable individuals who have been catalysts in shaping our current world?

Answer: Yes, child, we can discuss these issues

Question: Father, what are your opinions about Mother Teresa?

Answer: Mother Teresa, child, was a true and best example of goodness. She was the epitome of all humanity. Her care and concern knew no bounds and she worked long and tedious hours selflessly. A very kind, loving and trusting person, she felt remorse toward anyone in need, pain and affliction. She was a true Sufi in all aspects. She is to be revered here on this Earth Plane. Her accomplishments have made her an extremely evolved soul in the hereafter.

There are very few if anyone in comparison. She is true love for all to see and acknowledge. A child who endured much, she is one of God's most beloved.

Question: Can you tell me about Martin Luther King?

Answer: Mr. King was a man who fought for the Truth. He was furious about the state of his people in a racial dominated era in America. He knew that all children were God's most precious creations, and abhorred their mistreatment. He tried in vain to bring about justice in a very cruel and unfair society. It was a time of great turmoil, cruelty, frustration and torment of those people. What was the point? All children are God's children despite the color of their skin.

The Americans have much to learn and assimilate. He was a fighter and he was dedicated to his cause. A man noteworthy of his causes, he should also be revered and recognized for his humane actions and beliefs. He was wrongfully assassinated, and his loss is still felt in the hearts of his people today. An evolved soul, he is cherished for all he tried to do.

Question: Can you tell me about Mohammed Ali Jinnah, the original founder of Pakistan?

Answer: He, child, was a man who sought the rights of the Moslems in a much dominated Hindu society. He knew their plight within this society and wanted justice for them. He also knew that having a separate state would allow them to live a more peaceful existence. His efforts proved fruitful at that time and they do have a state of their own. However, the continual dislike between the two factions continues today with no point.

There is no need of racial barriers or ego driven attitudes. It is hard to fathom that there is so much dissent among individuals with the same skin coloring. Again, what are the gains, and what is the point? Children are killing children uselessly, child, and for what logical reason?

Question: What are your opinions of President Nelson Mandela?

Answer: A very humane, kind and understanding individual, he sought justice for his people's cruelty imposed upon them. He suffered tremendously in his fight for justice, but never gave up hope. His perseverance and tolerance are truly commendable. He is truly honorable and loved. His attitude and kindness are exemplary. A very noteworthy individual, he will remain in History as an example to all that follow him.

Question: What can you tell me about Albert Einstein?

Answer: Einstein, as he is called, was a genius. He was determined to prove his theories and help mankind with new scientific discoveries. A notable individual, his quests led him to believe that all discoveries were rooted in God, and that Science and Religion had no differences, and man was only a small part of this Divine Essence and creation. He became enthralled and in awe of God and all that he had created.

His discoveries were beyond his time and there will not be a scientist in comparison today to him. He was not only a scientist, but a humanitarian to all races first and foremost. He did not believe in race distinction and wanted to help with new findings all the time. He was truly troubled at mankind's plight and their need to empower.

Question: What can you tell us about Mahatma Gandhi?

Answer: The great Mahatma was a very kind, considerate and humane individual. He did not like the plight of his people under the British rule. He wanted and advocated a pluralistic society. He suffered by example to prove a point to both his people and mankind. He was very successful in his mission and was revered by all. A noteworthy individual as well, he will always be remembered throughout History. Unfortunately, his aim in having a pluralistic society was and is not met. He cared about all races of people and tried to make this a public fact. His attitude of nonviolence was truly exemplary of how God's children have to behave in any given situation.

Question: Lastly, Father, can you give us your opinion on King Hussein of Jordan?

Answer: King Hussein, was a man unlike any other. A kind, understanding and humane individual, his pacifists' ideas were not sought. He tried to bring peace in an era that was very rigid. His efforts were not met, heard or taken seriously. He was a man above all in his time. He tried, in his ailing health, to help the Moslem world be recognized and to bring about an end to the unnecessary blood shed of the Palestinian people. He was deeply hurt and felt that his dismissal by leaders of the world was terribly unjust. He was treated unfairly and unkindly by many leaders and was terribly disheartened. Very few, if any, individuals like him will go the "extra mile" for their own kind. A man whose family is a direct descendant from the time of my ancestors; I am truly proud of him and his accomplishments. His name will stay forever throughout History and he will be revered by many and for generations to come.

Thank you, Father, that was truly inspirational.

Child, many noteworthy individuals have come onto the Earth Plane to benefit mankind. Some of these individuals have been beneficial in their efforts, whilst others persecuted for their ideals. When will mankind ever learn? The ego-based individuals are at a stage in their lives that they will have thousands of victims destroyed at any cost, and at others expense. There is no gain, but continual injustice for the innocent masses. These self-serving individuals forget that they, like all others, are also part of God's creation.

Go, child, with peace, clarity and above the benefit of bringing about the Truth. Thank you child.

November 12, 2002

Question: Were the events that transpired on September 11, 2001 meant to happen?

Answer: They were transgressors and evil doers, my child. All the children that died suffered a shameful death.

Question: Was this event in any way pre-ordained or planned?

Answer: Death is not always preordained. This was a murder by far, by all means. The people that died, some were meant to die, some have become martyrs and others had a lot of their karma relinquished due to their untimely death.

Question: Is life generally not pre-ordained?

Answer: Sometimes certain aspects can change a situation. Situations like environment, stress, unhealthy eating habits, bad vices like drinking, smoking and taking drugs. It all depends.

Question: What happened to their families after the tragedy?

Answer: The grieving and the loss of their dead gave them wisdom they did not have before. Some had to learn lessons and some had to obtain compensation through the death of their kin. No one is left to mourn without some benefit.

Question: What happened to the orphaned and single parent children?

Answer: The bond of the single parent to their children will bring them closer than before. For the orphaned children their kinfolk will take care of them. We always give support in different ways. No one is left without any aid. America will compensate the children of the demised kin. They are a land of offering and will take care of their people.

Thank you, Father, I am truly blessed. This is really you and not my imagination?

No, my child, you are blessed. You have been searching for the Truth, and the search for the Truth is the search for God. Go in peace, child.

November 13, 2002

Question: Father, can you tell me about creation, Atlantis and Aliens?

Answer: When there was nothing, there was God. Everything came into being through him alone. There are many universes. God's creation knows no bounds and is continuous. Aliens, as you call them, are more evolved beings in other universes. They have come to mankind many times to help in their evolution. Atlantis was a very civilized nation that was helped by these Aliens who tried to give their civilization much advancement. The priests or the elders of that society had a lot of knowledge, and their life style was very highly advanced. Ego, pride and vanity are the barriers that destroy since the beginning of time. Throughout history, it has destroyed many civilizations. Atlantis drowned with the ego of those superiors who tried to control the masses and abuse their powers.

Question: Were there any survivors?

Answer: The ones from Atlantis and Lumeria moved onto other places including Egypt, and helped the priests there learn many mathematical and scientific solutions, far advanced than it was possible in that time.

Question: What is the reason for alien abduction?

Answer: Not all civilizations have total compassion. They are a superior race and most are spiritual and very advanced. The unity amongst them is very exemplary. Like mankind uses animals to experiment, they are trying to see what people are all about. A lot of visitors have come to help, to heal and to enlighten.

Thank you, Father.

Bless you child. Go in peace and love.

November 16, 2002

Question: Father, can I ask about Prophet Jesus and his death? Can I put this in the book?

Answer: Yes, you may. I would like both the Moslems and Christians to understand Islam's stand on this issue.

Question: What really happened?

Answer: Child, his time for death was and is a major turning point to Christianity. The Truth was that Jesus was a beloved prophet of God's. Jesus, who knew that he was about to die, was told to go into hiding. There was another thief whose face was changed by God to look like Jesus. They mistook him as Jesus and had him killed instead. Jesus' soul departed at the same time. God will never allow a killing of his beloved.

Question: What about the saying "Father, please forgive them for they do not know what they are doing?" Did Jesus not say those words?

Answer: Because the thief had taken on the image of Jesus, Jesus, who died prior to the thief, came onto his being and told him how elevated his soul would be, as the thief was being killed in place of him. Jesus was talking to the thief in spirit form and explaining to him how ignorant men were, and how Earth bound their thoughts as well. The man thus spoke those words knowing how great a place he would have in the hereafter. Understand, child, before his death this thief was absolved of all of his sins. Jesus, took with him this soul in the hereafter, and, whilst dying, became an exalted and very evolved spiritual being. Those that believed in Jesus and thought that he was being killed, were given this assumption to be in their hearts. Jesus and his spirit were ever present and what they felt was his ambience near the thief.

God, in his mercy, would never ever, child, have or allow his prophet to die in such a horrendous way.

Question: What happened to Jesus body?

Answer: Understand, child, when he passed on, no one was to know that he died differently than what had really transpired. His body, with the Help of God, had its atoms dissimilated so that it "disappeared" or disintegrated. God enabled this to happen so as no one would have a proof of his real death.

Thank you, Father.

Go with understanding, wisdom and peace, daughter.

November 17, 2002

Question: Did Ramses, King of Egypt, really drown in the parting of the Red Sea, as revealed in the Holy Quran?

Answer: His economy was labor based, on slaves. We showed him many signs and even God's wrath was of no avail. He did not heed.

Question: Did he, in his anger, follow Moses and his followers into the desert?

Answer: Yes, child. He went after Moses to get his slaves back. The sea had parted for Moses and his followers. When Ramses tried to follow, God had the sea returned to its normal state.

Question: Did he ever realize that God was the true God?

Answer: Child, he did. But, his ego and vanity were not going to go unheeded. He was the cause of much bloodshed and uprising. His laborers and slaves were mistreated. Families were unhappy and his land suffered because of his foolish pride.

Question: Can you comment on his wife Nefertiri?

Answer: Ramses had many wives, his favorite was Nefertiri. She was intelligent and proud.

Question: Did she not tell him to heed to the truth?

Answer: She did, but his vanity knew no bounds. She gave up and was angry when her first born died.

Question: Could she not try and make Ramses come to terms with the fact that he alone was the sole cause of all the first born children's deaths?

Answer: Not initially, she blamed Moses for that. She encouraged Ramses in the end due to their child's untimely death.

Question: What became of Nefertiri after Ramses died?

Answer: She, with the help of the priests, tried to rule, but was eventually overthrown.

Question: Was Ankhanaton, another Egyptian Pharaoh, really monotheistic?

Answer: Yes, he believed in God, but it was not God, but the Sun. He felt that all life was ordained and enriched and controlled by the Sun. He also believed that he was the link to this One Sun God and made everyone move to his new city.

Thank you, Father.

Remember child, Egypt was in a time where status quo and position held supreme. Negative forces control and continually contaminate. They destroy the mind and eat at the soul.

God bless you, go with peace

November 18, 2002

Question: In Islam we hear a lot about Mansur Al Hallaj. Can you tell me who he was and what he was like?

Answer: Child, he was an ascetic. He was a pious man who sought no recognition from society. He had very little worldly goods. His generosity knew no bounds.

He sought the Truth and suffered both physically and emotionally. He went and learnt from many masters and realized how close he could come to God. His path was one of staunchness and he did not fail despite all the odds and the obstacles. In those days, having conversations like the ones we are having were considered blasphemous. He narrowly escaped death many times with God's help. He persevered for the love of God. He wanted to attain complete and total annihilation.

Question: Was Jalelludin Rumi one of his teachers and how did Mansur Al Hallaj achieve oneness with God?

Answer: Yes, Rumi was able to help him in Sufism, and the ways and methods of being an ascetic in all respects. He was convinced that there was more, and he knew that he had to give up materialism totally and try to live a complete spiritual life. He himself became a teacher and through his meditation transcended into God. He was now complete and saw only God in everything around him. In those days, this was against the norm of behavior and he was totally spurned.

Question: Was it true he had insects and other creatures living in his clothing? Did they affect him?

Answer: Yes, he did have these creatures living in his cloak. They however did not inflict any harm to him. These insects knew he would enable them to stay with him. He or God, being one, knew that all was his creation. It bothered people when they saw this, but his point was that as long as God was with him, even creatures that normally harmed one would not harm him, even though they were close to his skin all the time.

Question: Did he have many followers?

Answer: Yes, he was able to convince quite a few and was totally shunned and ridiculed by others. His patience and fortitude knew no bounds.
He needed very little and God always made sure he was provided for. His death was an example of all those who mocked him; what a great person he was and how he transformed into "oneness." He was a beautiful, remarkable and very exemplary soul. He was a soul that has proven worthy beyond time and space and infinity. His name will continue forever in the Moslem and even in the Christian world.

Question: Truly spectacular. What about his family, did he not have an obligation towards them?

Answer: He made sure they were financially taken care off. He had land and a dwelling for his wife. He sat and talked to her telling her of his goal and path he was to choose. She was kind and understanding and loved him enough to allow him his freedom. Yes, he did see his son many years later and was proud of his upbringing.

Question: Can we discuss the benefits of meditation?

Answer: A human being is always given his spiritual cleansing through his trials and tribulations in life. However, meditation has to be done as it spiritually connects the spirit to God, the Creator. It transforms the person's well being in all ways and gives them "soul awareness." Meditation and prayer and a life of humanity, love and brotherhood is the "Truth" and a road to the right path of Nirvana.

Thank you, Father.

I love you child, go in peace and awareness.

November 19, 2002

Question: What is the motive behind Ossama Bin Laden's terrorism?

Answer: He is an evil doer in all aspects. He uses the religion
as a base for his actions. He has no real belief. He is a total trans-
gressor. A dark man whose only motive is revenge. He spares
no one for his quest.

Sometimes, when our minds are so tainted with anger we do
not see beyond. The Palestinian situation is there, but God by
all means did not appoint anyone to decree such an atrocity.
God is kind and benevolent. How can an omnipotent father
be so unjust? He didn't create his children to have them destroyed. Understand that the Gaza strip situation has been issue
for years, despite many attempts for a peaceful resolution. The
huge number of deaths in that area is really not necessary. Life
for a life is not stipulated in any religion. Revenge is never an
issue. It just is not correct. Did it resolve anything? Did the situation disappear? What did it accomplish?

Question: How do you feel about the Americans in all of this and their part in Global peacemaking?

Answer: Being a super power they dictate much decision making. They have been for years. They are generally weary of having to face consequences for their actions. However, they are also responsible for the global situation at present. They have been aware of the Palestinian problem for nearly 4-5 decades and never seriously had it resolved. Their motives were only those that helped their self interests, and not one of those afflicted people. Their decision making was only self-serving.

Question: What are your opinions of the American attack on Afghanistan?

Answer: They felt that they had been invaded despite their best security measures. It was also an ego problem. They had to show the world that they had to maintain their status as a world power nation. It was a question of "how could we be attacked?" As they keep claiming constantly, it was totally 'surreal'. No, it was not necessary to keep bombing. The ground troops would have sufficed. However, looking back, it didn't bring the perpetrator to justice, but only hurt the innocent masses and made many thousands homeless and in total dismay.

Question: What do you feel about the current climate in the world today?

Answer: Well, as far as terrorism is concerned, it will continue to destroy various areas in different continents on Earth. Again, what place is really safe anymore? The U.S. President again is on "attack," but he fails to understand the underlying reason of their attacks and demands. It is a good idea to hit any issue at its core, rather than ignoring the substance or basis of the terrorist attack. A terrorist mind is one tracked, black and white. You either meet their demands or get destroyed. This is what he has to try and resolve. Attacking on being attacked is no answer. It definitely is a not resolution. Mr. Laden is not even a fanatic, but a condemnation of Islam and the Muslim Umma. His hate has no bounds. His inhuman actions are everything against the principles of Islam. The sad issue at present is how tormented and scared my children are. They are being in the forefront and have had to pay for society's condemning them as a race, with no real fault of theirs. Also, understand that the world is not really educated about Islam and its true essence. These terrorist attacks are somehow compounding the fact that Moslems are a violent race. I taught peace, brotherhood and love. When did I ever, in all my teachings, ever say anything about resorting to any form of violence? It troubles me to see how my teachings, beliefs and sayings have been misinterpreted to suit any leader of the Umma. This disturbs me greatly.

Thank you, Father.

Go in peace child and in love.

November 20, 2002

Question: Father, some individuals are so materially bound that they will do or resort to anything at anyone's expense. What is the reasoning behind this attitude?

Answer: This individuals' chakras or soul focus are at the lower levels. They are more materially than spiritually focused. Satisfying their basic needs is their prime motive in life. It can be quite dangerous if it gets out of hand. It would be destructive. It tends to be biological or physiological. If the tendencies are abnormal, the individual needs to seek a therapist.

Question: Father, can you explain Islam's take on smoking, drinking and the taking of drugs?

Answer: Islam, child, has always forsaken these habits. These habits are dangerous to one's health. Moderation aside, these habits do not prove or lead to any advantage. Remember, child, smoking destroys one's internal organs, as the chemicals in a cigarette are most harmful to one's body. We have to comprehend that modern society drinks for social reasons. Even though a very small amount is not harmful, but, every sip, even if it is red wine which does help the heart, does destroy the brain cells. If, however, one had to take it for medicinal purposes, in small quantities, then one has no choice but to consume this. But, as one's body is the temple of the soul, it is better to persevere. The word "sin" attached to these items in question is not factual. God never said that drinking is a "sin" or smoking is a "sin." It becomes a danger when addiction takes place. These habits are addictive, if continued, and if not controlled, can destroy one emotionally, physically and mentally. They can harm those around them and endanger their families as well. The future of their health is at stake and it is not wise to indulge in these habits, especially around one's children. Abuse of these habits does indeed destroy the soul.

 If a person does engage in drinking say one glass, perhaps, say once or twice a year socially or very occasionally, one has to be careful to be lured into liking these habits. They are habit forming. Smoking, by all means, is very wrong as it destroys most outrageously. Drugs, in particular, are the worst substance use any mortal can partake. It destroys the brain cells and disables proper concentration, which is especially warranted in an age where the intellect is so highly demanded.

Spiritually, a healthy body and mind are needed for meditation. It is only through meditation that a soul can come close to one's maker or the Divine Source or God. **This is very essential for all human beings to understand and most definitely to grasp.**

Question: Can you now explain, please, Islam's ideas on sex and the concept of "living together?"

Answer: Sex, originally, a concept for procreation, was ordained for two people who truly loved and wanted children from their bond. It is treated very frivolously and taken for granted. Marriage, although not a religious act, is a partnership contracted amongst two people who vow to be loyal, trusting, caring, respectful and loving toward one another.

This unity is highly respected in God's eyes. It is a unity of body, mind and soul. The sexual pleasures and abuse of today are totally without any virtue.

God, made the human body to be acknowledged, nourished, cared and most of all respected. When there are two consenting adults who feel that their relationship will bond into a fruitful future, it is well advised that this bond will be without any detriment. Remember that as the two people commit themselves in a relationship their trust toward each other is important.

However, in situations where people have different partners for pleasure, it is a misuse of one's body. There is no real love here, but just temporal pleasure. The proper pleasure derived from a union of equal minds and souls are more beneficial. The human body, a temple of one's soul, is to be highly respected. God, made men in his image, so self-respect is very crucial.

Temporal pleasures will never be completely satisfying for any person, as it is like hunger that consumes one until that need is satiated. It is best to find true love, if one is lucky, and be content.

The concept of "living together" is again like a temporary contract. Here, the issue of children comes into play. Decisions also have to be made on the future of each partner before two people decide to "live together." Again, keep in mind trust, fidelity and respect for each other is important. This temporal "contract" has to have a benefit for all intended parties. In the modern world, mortals fear marriage and the consequential "divorce" stigma. I, child, do understand this. However, to me marriage is a solid bond between two people, where two people feel that the commitment has to be taken seriously.

Still, there are numerous marriages that are horrendous and abusive in every way, which are unhealthy and mentally unsafe for the partners and the children involved.

Divorce, in Islam, is allowed, and proper provisions should be given to the spouse. The visitation rights of these children should be encouraged tremendously. The fundamental beliefs of taking children away from a mother are very wrong, child.

No child should be brought up without parents. However, in divorce situations the children should be able to have equal participation from both parents. It is crucial for the developing years and allows a healthy environment for them. Today, a lot of troubled children grow up to be misbehaved and abusive adults. This is harmful to society as a whole. No mother should be kept away from her children. She is the mother of a son or of a daughter. It is most unfair to bring up children unequally. A boy or a girl should be treated equally and with compassion. They should be taught morals, compassion, understanding, consideration for all and most importantly respect for all of God's creations.

These issues, daughter, are very critical and are a serious matter in today's climate.

I am extremely distressed to see the plight of women in general and especially, in male dominated societies. Did their mother not give them birth? Is she not a female? Have they not the same blood as their sisters? God created all living things equally and with equal intellect.

Father, I am so happy that these issues are being addressed.

Child, the Truth shall always prevail, and so will love. Love, again is all there is. Go with health, and blessings of no distress or worries in your life, child. Take care of yourself and remember one's health is an important factor.

Thank you, Father, I love you.

I love you too, child, oh precious one.

November 21, 2002

Question: A personal question. How did Angel Gabriel appear to you and what was your initial reaction?

Answer: It was a beautiful sound. I was shocked, amazed, scared, but most of all in total awe. He was pure radiating gold light. It was quite overwhelming and he assured me that it was not a frightening experience. He was kind and comforting. His presence was all peace and love combined. It was truly a remarkable and beautiful experience.

Question: Were you apprehensive in the fact that God chose you to be the next Prophet?

Answer: Absolutely, it was a very surreal experience. I was at first petrified. Remember that I was a mortal like you, child, and quite taken aback. I was shaking and once he revealed his message, I could not wait to run and tell Khadija my experience. What would she think? Would she believe me? Would she think I was crazy or hallucinating?

Question: How was her initial reaction?

Answer: She was concerned about my shaking initially. She sat me down and quietly asked me to go over all the details slowly. She tried to console me, as I was really scared. It's amazing how easily she believed in me and stood by my side. She trusted me completely. She was always the supportive, motivating and concerned wife. Her kindness knew no bounds. She helped my self-esteem and reassured me tremendously. I knew I had a mission to fulfill and she would always stand by me to the end.

Thank you, Father for your insights.

Go in peace, child. Have no fears and be more trusting in God

November 23, 2002

Question: Father, what do you think of terrorism?

Answer: The mind is an instrument, which allows one to use or help ascertain our points of view. When we feel a certain view, we perceive it and feel it is our way and that is the Truth. ***The fanatics use my name and God's name in vain. Killing, rioting or fighting was never my way, child. When did I ever profess or teach that hurting another human being was justified, no matter what the cause, especially when it is done in religion's name? Never have I wanted to have such mass turmoil and injustice done. I have always sought peace and peaceful measures.***

Question: What do you propose?

Answer: Understand that Islam and my teachings were not done for those times alone. I have never acknowledged that justice should be sought or dealt with inhumanely. All children are from God. Peaceful resolutions and measures have to be taken. Surely, killing is not the solution. With so many scientific and technological advances, why do my children still behave like illiterates? Fanaticism is a state of one's wrongful ideals. An educated and wise man of integrity will understand how wrong the actions and words spoken are. If the intellect is used wisely, can it not provide viable solutions? Can we not understand that for every action taken there is most assuredly a reaction? Do they really think that hurting one another will bring about the Truth, peace and a solution? My children all over the world are suffering. The Moslem Umma and its fanaticism have to change and reform. My teachings have to be taken as basic grounds of understanding the roots of Islam. The mode of thinking and way of living has to change with the times. A lot of my way of thought today would be with the times. We cannot continue with archaic behavior patterns. This is destructive to the Umma as a whole. It affects everyone, Moslems worldwide. What is the real point? What solutions did their actions prove? Was it worth it? These are the issues we have to understand and contemplate when we do or take any action at all.

Do we realize and know the consequences and most of all what if we were faced in that similar situation ourselves?

Understand, child, any action taken or spoken has to be done with great deliberation and one that does not bring about repercussions. We, all together, have to look at situations from a global point of view.

Thank you, Father.

I wanted my children to set a worthwhile and good example, to be able to stand up and be proclaimed as a Moslem. I did not want anyone to be condemned taunted or misconstrued, especially ridiculed. Our actions again, child, only bring us to the forefront. What again was the gain, if any? Go in peace and in wisdom. The intellect should be used at all times for benefit, not for injustice and destruction. Go, child, most of all in and for love.

71

November 29, 2002

Question: I was watching a program, where this author Tasleem, the author of the book Meyebela, was condemning you.
Can you comment on her reaction and her anger toward you?

Answer: First of all, child, understand where her anger stems
from. She was brought up in a male oriented environment,
where she took to all kinds of abuse. She was raped by her relatives at a young age, and she did not quite understand the principles of life or Islam.
I never married Aisha at a tender age, nor did I molest anyone.
Respect to all human beings is something I cherish and value.
Human life, whether male or female, is God's creation and
should be respected and nurtured. Her anger toward me is not
correct as she is implying falsehoods. As I have revealed to you
before, the Burkha, veil and Hijab were put into practice only to
enable women to be respected and not to be taken advantage
of.
As I have always professed, with changing times comes changing attitudes. Education and women attaining it were my prime
goals. I could never ever hurt any of God's creations, let alone
my own brethren. I was given Nabuwat to teach mankind of a

fair God, and to take them out of paganism and cruel behavior especially to women, and to teach kindness and love to all creatures. I married my wives to support and protect them, not to take advantage of them. I never advocated the marriage of four wives as I said earlier; as to have more than one wife would mean having to treat each one with absolute equality.

If the leaders of Islam today teach a falsehood, it is not of my doing. I always wanted equality of the sexes. Cruelty, injustice, pain, suffering and intolerance are what I tried to diminish.

She is advocating falsehoods. I had always talked about fate, destiny, reincarnation, which I am sad to say, has been taken out of the Quran, and the concept of "reap what you saw."

Tell me, child, why would a benevolent Father want an unjust Prophet? A Prophet is there to assist mankind, not destroy it. Any pain or infliction onto another would only make me feel their pain. Why would I instill that on a creation of my Father's? Love is all there is. I have always professed this. It hurts me deeply that Islam, a religion that I had wanted of equality, love, unity, fairness to all and brotherhood to all men has come to this. Revenge is absolutely forbidden in my eyes. It serves no purpose.

Child, there is no anger, just a feeling of sadness to Tasleem. She has been falsely misled. Her teachings have been wrong, and she speaks without any proof or verification. It is a time where my children have to find solutions of peace and not uprising, terrorism and killing. I am very sad to see so many of my innocent people killed. Be of whatever race. We are all children of one Father. Peaceful resolution without ego, vanity and revenge is the only way to have a better future for our children and their future generations. Life for a life, my child, is not the answer. What is the point? How many killings will it take? Children are children. Are we not all from Abraham?

God does not want to have his children abhor each another. The world has become very unsafe and very evil. Everyone seems to be living in an environment where they feel can benefit themselves.

Why does society allow such atrocities? It is time the educated masses stand up to such behavior. When I was on the Earth plane, men treated women worse than cattle. The situation has not changed apparently. I tried to help make the world better with my teachings.

Evil doers, selfish and the self-centered male oriented societies take my religion and my name in vain and advocate such un-called behavior. God created men and women with the same intellect. All have to gain self-respect, kindness, appreciation and understanding. Look and do research on how I truly loved each of my followers, my children and in particular how I respected my wives and daughters.

Talking without proof is wrong and dishonest. If Tasleem is try-ing to bring justice to an already cruel male dominated society, she is correct, but using my name in vain, and with untrue and unproven facts is an outright lie.

None of God's Prophets have ever had anything but the better-ment of mankind in their mind. We have all suffered greatly and yet we are still condemned and blamed for any wrongdoing. It is better to remain ignorant than lay blame, especially if it is not correct. Always have proofs before any accusation is placed.

In life, child, often one needs a reason or a person to blame for their anger. I do not have any feelings or emotions of anger. I am spirit and can understand the human emotion. She has to try and search within before putting blame. Search for the truth. Look at Islam and its esoteric meanings. A good example of how she is not very learned is her theory of death and the soul. To her, there is no soul and death is the complete end.

Child, each soul is a definite link to God. He created each spirit, which is a part of him. We are all his "little lights" of his one big light. His noor or light is in every atom of his creation. When there was absolutely nothing or a void, there was HE.

He is above all else. Our misfortunes are not his doing. We are the bearers of evil and wrong doing. God created purely with such purity. Each soul was beautiful and devoid of any wrong or bad. Materialism, sex, greed, ego and pride have led many astray. They are the wrong doers. Remember we all have to account for our actions. ***Using words like 'jihad' and being pagans behind the banner of Islam and pushing the idea of revenge in the name of God is totally blasphemous.***

The world, from the time I left, has deteriorated drastically. It is not a peaceful world. No one feels happy or safe. I look with utmost sadness at the state of the Earth plane and all its occupants.

I want all to be able to live as one, to unite, to be free of racial barriers, to be free of pain, sorrow and any kind of or form of affliction. God's children should be a race of kindness, hope, love and above all peace. All the Earth's mishaps like earthquakes are due to mankind's energy.

If we all used our intellect and understood each other and resolved issues on a humanitarian level, the world would be better. Each person has to understand each other, care and truly try to help each other. Whether they are friends, parents, relatives or neighbors, aid each other.

Remember that we have to have hope for a better tomorrow, and this can only happen when we see the other person's despair and unhappiness. Always look at another's adversity and try and put oneself in it. This is the way to help alleviate so much suffering. Again, love and respect each other and be kind to one. another. Wrong and evil doing does not bring solutions. What did the action accomplish?

Human life is a life form to be cherished, nourished, loved, understood and enhanced. The self-esteem and self worth is very crucial. When these values are crushed, a very unhappy soul with a lot of rage emerges.

This then harms them and those around them. A soul in pain does not know any better. This is truly sad and causes me great disturbance.

Question: The only way mankind will benefit is with a change of attitude, right Father?

Answer: Yes most assuredly. Every little step in the help towards anyone's plight is a step in the right direction. Islam is a religion of peace not violence in any form or way.

Thank you, Father for your advice. I think that anyone without any proof, like Tasleem, should not advocate falsehoods.

Yes, child, ignorance, is not bliss in this case. I pray that she gain better wisdom and knowledge to make her comprehend the Truth. Her anger is eating away at her and the torment she has faced has made her an unbeliever.

Go child, with peace, love, blessings and the understanding of helping mankind. Go with kindness to forgive one and all. After all, love is all there is, child.

December 3, 2002

Question: Father, I read the book "Princess" by Jean Sassoon. In the book, we are given detailed accounts of how women in Saudi Arabia are treated outrageously. What are your opinions about this kind of treatments?

Answer: Understand, child, the Arab countries, in particular places like Egypt, Saudi Arabia and even India, the men think nothing of their womenfolk. This is a tragedy. I had never heard or seen such cruelty imposed before. My teachings have been totally misconstrued and misinterpreted after I left the Earth plane. It pains me immensely, to see how my daughters have had no say in their lives, and are being mistreated worse than animals. Remember, however, all of us account for our deeds, and these misdeeds will have to be paid for very gravely against each soul's actions. Yes, it is a very painful and cruel existence for these children. My heart goes out to them. I am truly upset that my own children would torture their own without any feelings of remorse.

Question: Yes, it is truly a shame. I do not understand why men do not view women equally.

Answer: A male dominated society only sees and does what it prefers. All else is immaterial. Their guilt is not even existent. They are evil doers and total transgressors. They and the Taliban are no different. That is what is most horrid. No Prophet taught such outrageous actions against any creature, let alone women. I never allowed for cruelty, adultery, children and women abuse. The only reason one could marry more than once, was if a man could treat his other wife in total equality. This is just not financially, but physically, emotionally and mentally as well. Has this been possible? **Yet, they take the Quran and treat the words to their liking** so they can have more than one wife. **This is most assuredly a falsehood and a terrible injustice.**

Thank you, Father, I am sorry to bring up such subjects

Daughter, this is an important issue. It has to be directed. The attitude of the educated masses has to change such cruel thinking.

Go with peace, understanding and love.

December 4, 2002

Question: Father, in the same book "Princess", they call for the castration of women's private parts in a cruel and painful manner. Is this necessary?

Answer: Child, first of all, as far as castration goes, I never ever heard of such cruelty imposed on my daughters before. The elders decided on such a drastic measure. Not only is this dangerous to a woman's health and well being, it leaves her in pain all her life. Second, I never ever declared hygiene to be so sadistic. Hygiene is the proper cleaning of one's body, not the cruelty imposed onto it by such measures.

I cannot comprehend how the elders of my Umma even contemplated such acts. What or who was to benefit from them? I am ashamed of such actions that only bring about terrible injustice on my children. It is absolutely and unmistakably a far cry from the kindness and consideration I was trying to impose onto a barbaric race. With education and technology being in the forefront, how can this be tolerated? This is beyond any human understanding. Will they not realize the implications upon their soul for such atrocities? God, our Father, is very sad and unhappy with the plight of women both in Arabia, and in the developing countries. Whether one is from Pakistan, Thailand, China or Yemen, all the women have feelings. Each one is a child of God's and each one carries in them his spark or soul. Heed all men, who commit such acts on the innocent, the ones in pain, the needy and the victims of such circumstance. Have you not death to look forward to? Would you like to be in their roles and feel their pain and affliction? How can such mass sorrows be unheard? Are these not children of your loins like your sons? Have they not your blood and feelings? Would you, men, be treated with even 1% of such actions, would you tolerate them? We all account for our deeds, will not you, men, understand this gravity of injustice?

Thank you, Father. The truth has to be revealed and understood. I only hope these men understand and change their attitudes.

Yes, child, human beings forget that death is not far. Our lavish lives and our concern for pleasures in the material world are going to disappear rather quickly. A young baby grows old quite rapidly and eventually is put to his grave. What did he accomplish in his lifetime? What does he have to show for his deeds? **These are important questions and have to be understood and addressed by one and all.**

Bless you child for helping my Umma understand the misinterpretations of Islam, a faith I wanted to bring with love and humility, which is being destroyed by the elders falsely. They too have to ascertain and understand how wrong their falsehoods have been.

Go with love and peace, child, remember again that Love is all there is.

December 7, 2002

Question: Father, what are your hopes and aspirations for this world?

Answer: Child, my biggest wish is for peace and love to all mankind. I do not want injustice to anyone, whether it is a human being or an animal. Respect should be given to all, every creed and to everyone, especially women. The old, needy and desperate should be both respected and cared for in every way. Technology is a blessing and a burden as well, daughter. It is also a health hazard in many ways. The present conditions of the world are horrific. Unless there are no peaceful solutions, nothing will improve. God gave man intellect to use to his best advantage. It is being misused and thus there are many evil doers today, daughter. The intellect should be used for the benefit of one and for others around them. Use it wisely, and for the purpose of attaining and giving wisdom, and in enabling others to grow spiritually. It is very sad to see that despite the fact that God created mankind intellectually equal, they are not a part of society's standards, especially in developing and fanatical societies where women are treated worse than animals.

We have to acknowledge that our daily lives do not last forever.

81

Shahnaaz

Death is always and should be topmost in our minds. We account for every single misdeed and good deeds. What will we show in the hereafter? We all have souls or the Divine spark in each and every one of us. God has the love of all his children and does not like the way his children treat and harm each other. The misinterpretation of the words of the Quran and the Bible have made a tremendous effect on the livelihoods of people.

The leaders of society proclaim truths that are falsehoods, standing behind the banner of religion and all the Prophet's sayings. For centuries, religions have been both a blessing, and their misinterpretation, a burden on society. These leaders, for their own benefits have brought about a falsehood that has caused much destruction.

Question: Are there no solutions to these atrocities?

Answer: Again, the educated masses have to bring about a "new age." A revolutionary age has to come into place where all the people feel like equals. As times change, so do the thinking, and questions have to be put on the validity of certain issues. Research should be done to ascertain facts. As no Prophet has ever approved of killing, why then do people do it? Questioning and peaceful solution making is the only way to improve these horrid circumstances.

I have always wanted a serene and peaceful life for my people. I never wanted strife between themselves and especially with others. The current Palestinian issue is outrageous and for what benefit? Did I ever forward revenge? What in the final analysis is the gain?

Why cannot the powerful leaders of the world try and help administer a united Earth with benevolence and kindness? Each should set an example for others to follow.

The Ecosystem of Earth is being destroyed. Again what is the point? Why must we sit back and watch without any action or any change? Why allow wrongdoings, falsehoods, corruption, greed and ego into our lives? Are we going to benefit with any of these in the hereafter? The Karmic Wheel of Life and reincarnation will only continue to misplace these individuals in lives that only destroy them. Again, what was the point?

Peace and peaceful measures are the only solutions. Remember love one another. Your wives, daughters and elders have much love and wisdom to offer. Do not treat them as lowly citizens or human beings without any status. Do not harm or hurt anyone in anyway including verbally. Revenge is totally disgusting; it only breeds more contempt. Remember "we always reap what we sow" most assuredly. Do not use the Prophet or God or the religion's name in vain for actions that destroy, or to benefit one or to harm others.

I love you, father, you are truly wise, loving and caring.

God and I love you, and especially for bringing and revealing the Truth to the people in mass suffering. We pray for each and every individual's plight. Their pain and anguish are our pain and anguish. We love everyone and all people. There is no exception; we all, all races are God's children. Never forget God is benevolent and merciful. He did not decree any misfortune or unhappiness. Our deeds from the past and the present bring about our current afflictions. Our intelligence should be used to help our plights and those afflicted. Remember as Jesus said, "do not unto others as you would not do unto yourself."

Go with love, wisdom and the Truth, child. Bless you.

December 9, 2002

Question: Father, is it true, that Prophet Jesus had proclaimed that you would come as a Prophet called Ahmed after his demise into this world?

Answer: Yes, child, he did. He said it twice and for all to hear. He made it quite clear that I would be a Prophet, God's last, and I would be from the East.

Question: Why was it not heard?

Answer: In those days, it was difficult for anyone to conceive that there would be another after Jesus. They totally worshiped him and assumed his role was the Son of God. They did not want to believe another Prophet would come and that also from the East. The scribes did not make it clear in the scriptures, of this revelation, for fear of the people not believing in another Prophet after him. They wanted his teachings to be above all the others. Unfortunately, the leaders of that society, felt that they could make the decisions for the best of that community at that time. Everything was written down which they felt was important, and the rest either misinterpreted or discarded according to their views.

Question: Was this not totally unfair to the teachings of Prophet Jesus?

Answer: Yes, he was highly disappointed. However, as we are not mortals, we are ever forgiving. He hoped that at least his fundamental teachings on humanity, love, compassion, brotherhood and equality would remain amongst his people.

Question: What happened to Mary Magdalene after Prophet Jesus death?

Answer: She lived a life of piety after she had become a follower of Jesus. She loved him as a Master and lived a very pure life till her demise. She knew the wrongs that had been imposed onto her, and she tried as well to teach many, and indeed even converted many as well. She was spiritually quite advanced and evolved when she came over.

Question: Was it true that after Prophet Jesus died he came to her in spirit form?

Answer: Yes, most certainly he did. She longed for him and missed his presence and teachings. She was much tormented and he knew that her only solace was to see him once more. He also came to show that the spirit lives on and never dies, and that he would be in all his followers' hearts.

Thank you, Father.

Shahnaaz

Child, each Prophet comes with a mission to fulfill. The sole purpose is to make mankind a better race and to love God and one another. Each person brings their special traits and a special way of teaching and giving wisdom. All are beautiful to listen and comprehend. All the Prophets are God's beautiful and caring messengers of his words.

December 11, 2002

Question: Father, why is that even though you proclaimed Ali to be your successor, not only did this not come to pass, but there was a dissection in your followers into two parts, namely Shia and Sunni?

Answer: I had already known when my time would draw near for my demise. I also acknowledged that not all favored Ali as Imam. There were many problems within my followers. I specifically called for the followers to accept Ali. A lot of the Moslems assumed that I had said this in jest, as he was also my son-in-law. I did insist that I was leaving behind my teachings being compiled as the holy Quran, and Ali as the Imam to be followed and to learn from. Nevertheless, child, not all followed my wishes. The jealousy toward Ali was what caused the dissent and the 'split' to happen. It saddened me very deeply that after I departed my wish had not been fulfilled.

You see, my child, my teachings are only successful if listened properly. When ego and jealousy are prevalent all senses cease to exist. All reasoning vanishes from the faculties. Those who did not listen were thoroughly brainwashed.

Question: That is very unfortunate as the line of succession would have continued and we all would have been one unified 'Umma".

Answer: Very true, and yes it is very sad. See, my child, when there are corrupt mortals who seek glory for the benefit of themselves, and at the expense of another, it is a terrible loss and makes for misfortune for so many souls. The corruption and affliction today is due mostly from this issue. Had the reign of Ali continued we would not have such atrocities being put onto my children. All the falsehoods and misinterpretations of the faith would not be prevalent as well.

Question: What of the Twelvers or Moslems who stopped following other Imams as they think that the 12th Imam is in hiding?

Answer: The world climate is one great upheaval and Ali, with his teachings, would have brought a new era then and now. The fraction that occurred was highly unnecessary. As for the 12th Imam, how can anyone who knows how truly and important an Imam is proclaim such beliefs? What reason is there for him to hide? Imam is not ashamed nor needs a reason for abdicating or hiding. This is a misleading and false truth. The followers again believed in nonsensical propaganda.

If my children, with God's given intellect, especially the educated masses of today, would try and understand this concept, they would, through their research on Imams and Islam and the esoteric way of life, know most assuredly this was truly a falsehood. Understand the fact that God, the benevolent one, is neither one to fear nor one to get "angry," but a divine essence that knows, understands and listens to all.

The Imam has the authority to guide his followers; to what is best suited for their needs in this ever-changing climate on Earth. As the years go by, so will the guidance and teachings to always benefit his followers, whilst always retaining my teachings and their fundamental meanings.

I find that this dislike amongst the Moslems, most disconcerting. It is hard to see so much anguish amongst all races, toward one another, but especially amongst my own children. The mere act of judging one another is truly a shame.

Question: There are Moslems called Ismailis, I am told, that do not fast the full Ramadhan, nor do they pray five times a day or make use of the Burkha or Hijab. They have been shunned by the Muslim Umma and they find it difficult to defend their stand amongst other Moslems.

Answer: Again, with the times, realities have to change. As I mentioned, the Burkha is not necessary for the women to wear. Fasting was done to benefit one from not only improper behavior, but to appreciate what God has provided for us for our sustenance. The current Ismaili Imam and his predecessors know that God will never inflict any hardship to any child. His guidance of how the ismailis should be guided on both a spiritual and material level attests to the Truth. I feel very greatly for the fact that Islam has two divisions. I have always loved Ali and did indeed proclaim him as the next spiritual guide after me, to no avail. Hence the differences. Understand, that the Ismailis have kept with this following to their present Imam. He is purity in true essence and the Ultimate Truth. Blessed are those that have been led by Ali and his direct descendants. The Ismailis are an intellectual and exemplary group that tries to keep a balance both esoterically and exoterically. There are those in their community that are pure Sufi in thought.

Shahnaaz

Thank you, Father.

Child, the understanding of our principles and values of Islam, is crucial, but, as I said with the changing times, guidance changes as well.
Go with blessings and thank you child for bringing out the Truth. Truly bless and love you.

December 17, 2002

Question: Father, can you tell me what your predictions are for the future of the world?

Answer: Child, first and foremost, the mental capabilities of mankind are always a challenge. There are a lot of uneasiness and unrest in the world. People do not feel safe and secure, child, as they did say 10 – 15 years ago. This is due to all the unrest and upheaval in the world today. We have to understand that the world needs justice, compassion, love and most of all security. What next, will be a question so prevalent in everyone's minds.

Well, child, the future is grim. Many unfortunate things that are going to happen will take place that mankind has not and cannot imagine. At the current time, Iraq is under much scrutiny, but what the Americans cannot see, is that there is another, what seems a non threatening nation, brimming to come into view. A small nation that has been misunderstood and taken for granted. I am talking, child, of North Korea. Yes, child, North Korea. This small nation has developed much artillery and arms than any nation thus far. If any nation should be scrutinized it should be North Korea. They are going to be mankind's worst enemy. They will slowly march into other lands seeking a new form of a livelihood. They are communists with no compassion or feelings and will fight for their own good at the world's expense.

They will join forces with Russia and try to awaken the great powerful nation of America. They should not be taken lightly. This will start very slowly from the end of 2003 and 2004 onwards. They will bring forth, till about 2025, a world of great uneasiness and total unrest. Peace, religion, sanctity and compassion will diminish. Material pleasures and greed will be the prime motives in this era. It will be a terrible era and bring about great harm and injustice.

I love all my children and want to forewarn them that the temptations will be many, and so many fears will abound. It will be an age where shame, respect and concern for mankind will not be important at all.

My children please, please heed my words carefully. Please keep firm in your beliefs of God, compassion, love and kindness to each other. Do not let their socialist ideas and controlling factors change your mode of thinking. Stay with your ethics, your conscience and your beliefs in humanity. Have faith in God and the belief of overcoming the dark side.

God, our Father, is loving, benevolent, kind and merciful. Your belief in him will give you strength and courage to fight this adversity and triumph. God, will indeed, help those on the light side. The souls of the dark side are doomed in the hereafter. They will suffer tremendously.

Life, is only a small passage to eternity. Heed my children, and listen well.

As long as you have love, unity, brotherhood and kindness, you will not let their negative attitudes affect your thinking. Keep strong to your ethics and principles of what God seeks from mankind. Show mercy, not selfishness, show compassion and kindness, not ego, vanity, lies and greed. Heed, all children, please be assured that this tragedy is upon Earth!

Question: Father, it is hard to fathom that a small nation like North Korea will bring about such change in the future.

Answer: Yes, the lesson here is to never underestimate anyone or any nation. If one were to leave the smaller nations unnoticed, especially ones that seek empowerment and revenge, this is what happens. They have been in planning stages for a long time. They are ready to strike, and a strike they will. This is my forewarning to you.

Thank you, Father, for your foresight and forewarning.

Child, one must pay close attention. This is a critical matter. The Moslems are under scrutiny, especially when all of my children are far from being the culprits of destruction. The main destroyers are yet to come to overthrow the world. They will come quickly and swiftly and move toward America in force.
Their arms and weapons are abundant. They should be checked and inspected like Iraq. The world is not going to be a safe haven at all. Our children and the future generations will have much discontent and despair. It will be a totally changed existence for all. Only your faith and trust in the Truth will help you stay in peace.
There will be many mishaps and painful incidents yet to come. Many questions will arise as to why they are the ones. The quiet and unheeded ones of North Korea are going to show that they have to be noticed. Unfortunately, this race of people will not bring any forms of safety for the world. They are a selfish race and seek only their own means of existence. They want power and want to be noticed and heard. They feel they are a nation to be reckoned with.
Many supernatural events will also take place. A Comet will land

on Earth and will cause some destruction. This will be take place around 2004 –2005.

Mother Earth has undergone many changes, and all the unfortunate incidents being affected to mankind will be due to all the negative auras from misdeeds, acts of evil and cruelty imposed from one person to another.

What is the point of inflicting pain without justice being sought? Why do men continue to treat women so unkindly and unfairly? Why does the rich torment the poor? Why are there still people being treated as slaves or worse?

Many painful afflictions and sorrows continue toward my children all the time. This is truly devastating and uncalled for. I am very sad to see my teachings taken for granted and highly misinterpreted.

I have always felt the need for the respect of all of mankind and in particular to my daughters. Never did I allow for them to be stoned, killed, jailed or treated unfairly. This is a grave deed done by men and fathers alike.

This is a terrible adversity to watch and behold. The allowance of my daughters to prayers was never forbidden in the mosques. Had my children listened to me and continued with the teachings of Ali, we would have been a peaceful race and nation with the Truth and full of love and compassion. The Quran has many parables and metaphors that were there to teach at that time. As times change, the archaic interpretations and misinterpretations have been taken out of context. This is outrageous!

Was not your mother a woman? Did she not nurture and feed you?

My male children have to learn to treat all God's children with respect and humility. Life is very short and all of my children are going to die someday.

Hear the cry of the painful souls who long for freedom, safety, for love and respect. Did not God create Adam and Eve out of his spirit? Did he give superiority to one over the other? Each was supposed to support, sustain and care for each other and for the upbringing of future generations with respect. Which Prophet of God's ever taught such atrocities?

Follow the Truth, my children and have humility. Listen to the pleas and hearts of those being afflicted. None of us have the right to harm another in anyway at all. When we harm another, rest assured, we harm God's creation and thus disrespect our Father.

The world, if they understood such behavior, would be a more peaceful place to live in. There would not be an issue of security and fear. All people would come together as one and understand, that God in is his mercy, loves us all truly, and through our actions would indeed assist us in our search for the Truth.

Please listen to my words, tomorrow can be brighter and better if our attitudes and actions were to change. All nations should come together for peace and harmony for the benefit of all creatures.

My prayers are always for the Truth and for those afflicted and in need. All my children, who are suffering and in pain, child, I feel their sorrow. I hear their pleas and unhappiness, and I know that with the new generation and the educated masses, the unfortunate cruelties will have to cease. I pray for all my children and for the end of suffering.

The world is truly in a state of grave unhappiness for so many of God's children. Poverty stricken and helpless children bring me so much sadness. It truly hurts to see young children being mistreated and sold in child labor, and to see other acts of cruelty imposed on them.

My child, I hope that all your writings, will shed a new light for humanity and teach them that for every action there is most absolutely a reaction. If they will not get their justice here, it will be in the hereafter. Remember for every misdeed there is a price to pay. All actions, deeds, words and thoughts are recorded and will be brought forth in the hereafter. No one on Earth is exempt from death. What will they have to show? Where will they hide? They have to heed now. Changes have to be done now, child.

Thank you, Father

Thank you, child, for all your efforts. Bless you, take care, go in peace and love, and remember to follow the Truth in all you do daily in your life.

December 18, 2002

Question: Father, can you tell me a little about your child-hood?

Answer: Well, child, it was an uneasy time for me to comprehend how I could not enjoy the joys of parenthood. My uncle was truly a loveable and remarkable man, and he helped me in all my endeavors. Yet, I felt sad at being alone. I used to contemplate all the time how others in my situation felt. It was this awakening in me that felt for the children of poverty. Despite the fact I had my uncle, I felt for those children, who had no particular relative to rely on as orphans. I questioned as to why some children had parents, wealth and whilst others had poverty and misery. I used to sit quietly in contemplation and question many things around me. Even as a child, I deplored injustice on any of God's creation. It used to hurt to see so much barbaric behavior amongst the adults and people's of the various tribes.

Question: Father, did you have many friends?

Answer: I did have many friends, but most of the time we conversed. I did play, but my mind was always questioning everything around me. I loved nature and everything in it and watched the birds, camels and stars and was fascinated at nature totally.

Question: Father, can you tell me a little about your youth?

Answer: I was a youth learning many business tactics of trade. I was fascinated at how different people traded, how business took place, the various different cultures and the whole business scheme of those days.

Question: You not only helped Bibi Khadija in her business ventures, but you married her as well. How did this fare in the society you were living in, especially since she was almost 15 years older than you?

Answer: I was literally in awe. Khadija proved to me and everyone that women were equal in intellect and in stamina. She could raise a home, have a family, be a business woman and at the same time have humility. She was to me as they say "par excellence." Her ability to understand, sympathize and analyze situations was beyond words. She not only had a keen business sense, but was an articulate woman of great wisdom and courage. She was the one who helped Islam come to being, and was the first convert. She trusted me completely, and remained faithful till she died.

She will always be revered amongst all women. She is an example to both men and women of today. Did I treat her like my chattel, slave or belonging? Did we not talk freely and give opinions about everything? She partook in all my affairs and I loved her despite our difference in age. Love transcends age and beauty. Love is the purity of the heart and the inner being. Khadija was beautiful both externally and internally, child.

Question: Can you tell me about your spiritual ascension to God, otherwise known as the night of "Meraj"?

Answer: Child, it was a most blessed night. Angel Gabriel did indeed take me in my spiritual state to my Father. The horse is a symbol, a metaphor. It is a divine ascension of the spirit to the Divine Essence. It was truly auspicious, child, as I also met my forefathers and other Prophets who had come before me. It was a glorious night and I knew after that night that God, my Father and beloved, were all there is. He is absolutely the most beautiful, bountiful, merciful and compassionate Father. He is the Creator, first and last. He is the most awesome Divine Essence, daughter.

Question: What is the real meaning of the Moslem term "Jihad?"

Answer: Jihad, child, esoterically, means struggle in life to sustain oneself in proper behavior or piety and to be able to get closer to one's Divine Father. It is the daily acknowledgment of our actions and deeds toward each another, and also how we perform our rituals in our daily lives. A Jihad should not be such an act that would harm or hurt any individual. I never wanted a Jihad to destroy or harm any individual in a worldly manner. This is wrong. Any type of killing or bringing affliction onto another is absolutely immoral and wrong. The only reason I had to go into Jihad or fight, in my time, was attaining, for my followers, that which was rightfully taken away from them. The atrocious killings that are prevalent today, and especially what happened on September 11, 2001, were totally uncalled for and unfounded. What did these innocent people in those towers have to give you after you destroyed them? Did it accomplish anything? Regardless of what my children think, the killing was wrong. Peaceful negotiations are the only resolution, children. Listen, children, as violence never was and never is or will be the means to the end. Never, ever. All children are God's children. We are all "people of the one book". What is the need for proving our empowerment onto one another?

Question: Thank you Father. That was very profound. Can I ask a different question? I want to ask about Bilal, who is recognized as the first Muezzin of Islam.

Answer: He was strong and faithful and had the most piety of all of my followers. I loved him truly and he was exemplary amongst men. His voice resonated and reverberated to the point that it brought tears to my eyes. He was truly a sight to behold. Here again, the Meccans took him to be of a lower human race, I deemed him superior to others. Was he not also of God's creation? His only difference was his skin coloring. Islam is equality amongst all men, regardless of their station in life.

Question: Can you tell me about Salman, who not only helped in translating the Quran, but also helped you in the many wars against the idol worshiper?

Answer: Salman, another beloved of mine, had searched for the Truth for many years until he converted to Islam totally. A very sharp man, his intellect and quick thinking had helped me in many wars we had encountered. He is truly exemplary and translated the Quran in many languages. Both Bilal and Salman were some of my favorites.

Question: Besides Bibi Khadija, you had many wivves. Did you have another favorite?

Answer: I loved each one equally. They all had special qualities and each had a fine intellect as well. I respected and cared for them all.

Thank you, Father.

Go in peace and humility, child.

December 19, 2002

Question: When we look at the current oil issue that is prevalent in the world today, and the fact that we might be running out of fossil fuel, do you think there might be other sources we could utilize that would be beneficial for us in the future?

Answer: There are already many technological breakthroughs that are coming about slowly. The leaders of the nations of the world are not ready to bring about these discoveries out of fear of having economic decline. There are currently many oil-based economies at present that would go into turmoil. Naturally the technological breakthroughs will have to be put forth, in the long run, with depleted resources. There will also be new forms of highly advanced transportation. By the next century, child, this will be prevalent.

Question: Can you tell me if there will be any major breakthroughs in the field of medicine toward Cancer, Aids and other life threatening diseases?

Answer: For sure, child. Science is on the verge of many breakthroughs. There will come a time when man will be rid of most diseases, but depression will be a major issue. The cure of mental illness will be the most important issue at that time.

Thank you, Father, for those words of wisdom.

Child, live life fully knowing that God is at all times by each and everyone's side. No one is ever alone. No prayer or thought ever goes unheard. God is all knowing and loving. Have faith in him only and pray for forgiveness, child. Bless you and may you always be happy.

Go with love and peace, child.

December 28, 2002

Question: Father, one of the most frequently asked questions concerns the consumption of Pork. Why does Islam forbid the eating of Pork?

Answer: Child, it is a combination of many reasons. Yes, in the olden days it was forbidden to ingest anything unhealthy for one's consumption, and for the protection of one's health. To-day, even though times have changed, there are other grave reasons. The Quran proclaims that we cannot eat anything that is close to human genetics or hormones. The pig's DNA makeup, and its hormones, is similar to that of the human makeup. This biologically makes it a deterrent. We cannot consume anything that has the same hormonal structure as the human body.

The pig, when consumed, actually over time helps in the deterioration of the human body, as it would be like consuming itself. The future health of one's body and its aging process is greatly increased as well. Many diseases have the chance to increase due to this consumption. Once again, child, as the body houses the spirit, it is imperative to keep it healthy and pure of unsuitable substances.

Thank you, Father.

Understand, child, the fact that the younger generations of to-day are educated masses who are constantly seeking the right answers. Their questions toward the Quran, its interpretations and my teachings will continue. It is an era of the intellect and needs to be addressed and the younger generations need solutions.

Remember, God alone created man and he alone is the one and only Creator. All others are only co-creators, trying to imitate or copy this ultimate creation. The ultimate source is his alone. Can they create without any DNA or molecular biological beginning? No, they need something to assist, a means to the end, child, no real beginning. God does not and did not need any help or aid. He just created out of void, and still went on creating. All others are copies of his creation. They will all have flaws and cannot compete with him. Mankind is not above God, their original creator, who if chooses, can diminish and destroy all without reason. He, however, is truly benevolent and knows that he gave mankind their intellect to co-create and their free will to do as they desire. He wants only love and harmony for all. All people are one brotherhood and he seeks all to be one. Children, go in peace, love and above all the hope of human understanding toward one another. Love is everything. Bless you.

January 12, 2003

Question: Father, throughout history, we notice that the Prophets, who have tried earnestly to bring about God's message, have always suffered at the hands of their people. Can you comment on this?

Answer: Despite the fact that they knew God was on their side, the beloved Prophets suffered at the hands of the mortals and with nature as well. This was because in each time period, their fortitude and endurance was put to test. Faith is not always easy to hang onto. Struggling and achieving spiritual success to be one with our Father was our ultimate goal. All Prophets were viewed as suffering, but they had the strength of God with them at all times. Only our faith, trust and complete conviction in God kept us from faltering, child. The difficult world of the mortals is not easy to sustain in without God, our Father's help and guidance. He alone knows all and he alone is the provider.

True faith can endure anything, daughter. Trust should only be in Him, as He is the one above all else. Do you think anything would subsist without his knowledge?

Question: Father, why does God not intervene?

Answer: Child, He does know all. However, a lot of suffering is due to one's destiny. Each Prophet knew he would forego much distress before he came on the Earth plane; as helpers of mankind, and as highly evolved Master Souls, they chose to come regardless. Our strong faith in our Father enables us to have the fortitude and conviction to continue through our perils in life.

Question: The Prophets surely had a lot of forbearance.

Answer: Yes, child, but as human beings, we also were emotionally, physically, financially, mentally and emotionally distressed. There were times when our distress troubled us tremendously. Our faith sustained us and God always encouraged, motivated and inspired us as well.

Question: What can you tell me Father about Angels?

Answer: Angels, are God's most precious first creations. They are beautiful spiritual beings with great illumination. They are all love and they bring forth God's love in their messages. Their love knows no bounds and they are constantly trying to help mankind at all times.

Question: Do they have hierarchies or special assignments? Was there really an Angel who fell from grace?

Answer: The Spiritual Realm knows no hierarchy. No one is above the other or higher than the other. Yes, each one has his own spiritual assignment. Azazil, as the Moslems know him, was the fallen Angel. He felt that he was above the creation of man.

Thank you, Father, that was very interesting.

Go in peace and love, child. Remember to always have faith in him, our Father. His love and grace is insurmountable. Trust only in him and rely only on him.

January 14, 2003

Question: Father, why is that despite how well our intentions, and how humane we try to be to others in society, we still get condemned, mocked, taunted and ridiculed?

Answer: Child, most people from time beginning are basically self serving. History will verify, the issue of empowerment over another person, country or point made, has always been at the crux of every decision. When the ego, combined with one's vanity and many insecurities come into play, one's rational thinking disappears. The lack of appreciation comes when the person who is viewing the other is feeling inferior, and the only way to feel superior is to either criticize or taunt them at any given opportunity. The principles of ethics and scruples are set aside and one's defending of their "so called' dignity becomes an issue. Also, child, culturally, men have always viewed women as intellectually inferior and with no good reasonable or sound judgment. This male dominating attitude stems mostly from their upbringing and their environment that they have established for themselves.

Question: What solutions do you propose?

Answer: The issue is of self-worth, child. If we feel we have the qualities that deem us intellectual and capable, the other's point of view is than quite invalid. Our self preservation of our self esteem can only be done with the knowledge that the others affecting us are not only unimportant, but not worthy of our self destruction. Any intellectual and reasonable person, child, will look at the total scenario and understand that whatever is said is for their deterioration. Every deed done against another does not go unheard or unseen, daughter. Each action is accounted for and all have to adhere to their actions someday. Every action has a reaction and is and will be dealt with. A lot of times, actions that are done, are done in sheer ignorance of the consequences. Even the most malicious acts have to have a reason. Understand, child, and contemplate on the person doing the wrong. Why or what is the motive that drives them to do the action? Are they noteworthy of their actions? Are they really substantial that the pains they inflict will affect us emotionally, mentally and physically? If one is in an oppressive state, what solutions or peaceful resolutions can be adhered to that situation?

Remember at all times, that each and every one of God's creatures is important and no one is special or above the other. If God, our Father, does not differentiate in all of his creations, who then are we as mortals to do this? No one has to take on burdens that are unnecessary and unimportant.

Thank you, Father.

Child, let no one affect our humility and integrity. At all times we have to preserve our self worth and self esteem. Our constant faith and hope in our Father, God, will give us the strength to be able to surmount any difficulty no matter how small or inconsequential it maybe. Always remain in love, and give love, and this always changes most environments we are in or the problems we are facing. Peace and harmony are the key issues, and trying to understand and decipher each issue is critical.

Go with love, peace, harmony, understanding and faith, child.

January 23, 2003

Question: Father, can you shed some light on the pious and honorable Dalai Lama?

Answer: The Dalai Lama, child, is a Buddhist. He has had to do great penance and be quite disciplined to attain his status. He had to endure hours of meditation and spiritual teachings. Many long hours of learning and deep thinking on various levels of mind control were put on him. He has read extensively and is well versed in the scriptures of the Prophet Buddha.

Question: What was it like to reach the stage of enlightenment?

Answer: To reach the stage of enlightenment, child, one has to be in total submission to God, and be submerged in the Divinity as well. The Dalai Lama is a much evolved soul, and has a high spiritual standing. His teachings are unique and he has much wisdom.

He, child is considered to be a great spiritual leader of the Buddhist community. His vast knowledge and understanding hold him high in today's standards. Unlike a Prophet, who is here to deliver God's message, the Dalai Lama is totally submerged in helping bring about goodness in mankind.

He is a great teacher and philosopher. He has great clairvoyant abilities as well.

Question: Can you tell me more about Prophet Jesus life here on the Earth plane?

Answer: Jesus, son of Mary, was of total piety. He was a kind, loving and caring individual since childhood. Throughout his childhood he did not like anyone inflicting pain on any of God's creatures. He was a very loving and considerate child; always obedient and he never complained about anything. He did not have much in the way of material pleasures, but he never complained. He grew up to be a man of great fortitude, forbearance and tolerance. His attitude in itself was exemplary. A quiet individual, he would sit in quiet contemplation at all times. It was in his youth that he was called to his duty of being a Prophet.

Question: He performed many miracles and helped many in their physical affliction.

Answer: Yes, child, he was always concerned about the down trodden and helpless individuals. He was of the Truth, and it was the Truth he sought and taught to his people. A serious youth, he never found true joy in the Earth plane. He was truly sad at the way mankind behaved toward each other.

Question: What happened to Mary, his mother, when Jesus decided to leave in search of the Truth?

Answer: She was utterly heart broken. She loved Jesus more than her own life itself; however, she also knew that he was here for God's mission. It pained her deeply to see him leave.

Question: It must have taken great fortitude to see him being crucified?

Answer: In her heart, she could not truly believe that he was being crucified. She knew that God could not hurt Jesus, whom he loved so much. She watched, but her heart and soul did not accept what she was viewing.

Question: What was Mary like in her youth?

Answer: She was a lovely child with a quiet temperament. She was a loner and always worked by herself. She was a great thinker and would sit in solitude looking at everything about her. She was complacent and very kind, and never hurt or harmed anyone or anything. A very hard worker, she always did her chores with great care and precision. She put her heart in everything she did. She cared for all those around her and loved her husband Joseph truly. Her greatest joy came from Jesus, who she was immensely proud of all the time. She also acknowledged the fact that she was lucky to be his mother.

Question: What was the Great Buddha or Prince Siddhartha like?

Answer: Prince Siddhartha had all the material comforts a child would desire. He was his parent's beloved child and he was totally spoilt. However, child, he was never arrogant or vain. He was a great learner and always questioned everything he learnt. He was admired by all that knew him. He was always concerned about the life outside the palace walls, and knew that there had to be more to his existence. He wanted to know about his creator and the way the world was created. His wife adored him and he had a beautiful son.

Prince Siddhartha had a restless nature and his soul yearned for more than his very constant life. He was startled to learn about mankind and all the various diseases and health problems. His questioning and extreme inquisitive nature forced him to leave his very content life to seek the Truth.

Question: Was it very difficult for Prince Siddhartha to live outside of the palace walls?

Answer: Initially, very much so. He persevered despite the odds. He suffered physically and understood the pain and affliction on himself. He knew what hunger, starvation and discomfort meant and especially poverty. His travels were quite extensive, and he gained knowledge about different people and their ways of life. He meditated extensively and realized that he did not have to torment himself to find the Truth. He learnt fast and evolved spiritually. He became a great Prophet of his time. He was a wonderful orator and teacher. His ideas and teachings are truly exemplary. His way of life was very ascetic and he changed and converted many to the Truth. He taught about life after death, and his views on reincarnation brought on a new light to the world. The world at the time was very materially inclined. He tried to change the attitude and thinking of his people and did it by example.

Question: Can you tell me about Prophet Moses?

Shahnaaz

Answer: Moses, child, was brought up in luxury. Adopted by Pharaoh's sister, he knew no hardship. He had abundance and joy and was given material comfort. Moses had a great mind and was a fast learner. As a child he was very astute and sharp. An obedient child, he never disliked or harmed anyone. He was kind and understanding despite his high rank. He had a great stature and his presence was always felt whenever he walked in a room.

Question: How did Moses feel when he had to acknowledge the fact that he was not Egyptian, but of Jewish descent?

Answer: Moses was very upset. He did not have any idea that he could be anything but an Egyptian prince. Once he learned the Truth, it took him a while to grasp at the concept. He finally undertook the task to search for his kin. He realized how the other half lived and he became a changed man completely. The material comforts of his life become unimportant and humanity and the understanding of human affliction came into view. He contemplated for hours on the meaning of life.

Question: Did the fact that Ramses, Moses childhood friend, make it difficult for Moses to confront him?

Answer: He knew Ramses and his vanity. He also felt the injustice of the labor class and slaves. Despite the fact that Ramses was his friend, he knew he had to maintain his stand on the Truth. He had complete and total faith in God and was not concerned about Ramses or Seth's opinion. His love for God superceded all else.

Question: What about his love for Nefertiri?

Answer: He loved her deeply, but his love for God was above all else, child. He knew that to love God was more important than a mere mortal.

Question: What was Nefertiri's reaction when Moses decided to leave his lavish life?

Answer: She was very deeply hurt and tormented. She also knew Moses was stubborn and would not change his mind. Moses was a person who had a strong mind set. Once he made up his mind, nothing deterred it.

Question: Did Moses feel that he had accomplished everything he had promised God?

Answer: Yes, he knew that he had worked very hard in helping his people get away from Pharaoh's afflictions. They were free and lived promising and fulfilling lives. He died quite peacefully.

That was truly fascinating, Father, thank you.

Child, all these great people are and were exemplary. They all brought much wisdom to the Earth plane and all were truly in love with the Truth and God. Each was beyond exemplary and continues to still be held in high esteem. Their knowledge and teachings are not only noteworthy, but also something mankind should follow and put to practice on a daily basis.

Child, bless you. I hope that mankind will see and appreciate these great souls who dwelled in the Earth plane at one time. The Dalai Lama is very much someone to be honored. Go child with peace, harmony, wisdom and understanding.

January 24, 2003

Question: Father, what is Islam's view on Religion and Science?

Answer: Child, there is no distinction. Science is today finding out what God had already created from the beginning. Each time there is a discovery; it is only revealing his magnificent creation. God's creation is always continuing and knows no bounds.

Question: Is the Big Bang Theory the real theory of Evolution?

Answer: Yes, most assuredly. When there was a void, there was only HE. God then said, "BE" and there was an explosion, which took place, causing atoms and molecules to combine. Earth and its galaxy are only one of God's creations. There are many planets and many galaxies, child. Each galaxy is beautiful and unique.

Question: Father, how would you describe God?

Answer: The most omnipotent, most benevolent and most merciful Divine Spirit of all. He is above all else and knows no barriers of time and space. There are not enough books, poems, writings, descriptions and sayings to fully grasp his magnificence.

Question: What was the necessity or need to create?

Answer: God, a true and blessed treasure, wanted to be known as revealed in the Quran. He wanted to experience his creation first hand through them both physically and on an emotional level.

Question: So in other words, through his creation, God then experiences all feelings and emotions?

Answer: Correct, child. That is why it truly bothers him when there is injustice being said and done. He actually feels every moment anything that is taking place.

Question: Can God not prevent all this from happening?

Answer: No, each creation has their destiny to fulfill. In an addition child, the free will enables one to do as one chooses and pleases.

Thank you, Father.

Go with blessings and peace. The world and its many technological breakthroughs are only due to Allah's intellect that he has given to mankind. It does not give one the right to be vain in discovery or the ego of discovering new horizons and inventions. All is due because of Allah, child. He and he alone, enables discoveries to happen at certain times in different centuries for mankind.

January 25, 2003

Question: Father, what are your opinions about President Saddam Hussein?

Answer: He is a man, child, full of hatred and revenge. He is a self-serving individual, he only cares about himself. His cruelty and injustice to his people are absolutely atrocious. To him everything he does is a means to an end. His country suffers much turmoil today. He is an individual that loves to rule regardless of how ruthless he comes across. His ego and vanity know no limits and he is totally unethical in thought and action.
 He never was and is a dishonest individual. He does not reveal more than he wants to despite the consequences.
His hatred toward the Americans is so great that he does not care of any consequences. He feels that the Americans have no right to invade his country and pry.

Question: Do you think war is imminent?

Answer: Mr. Bush is very serious about his disarmament policy. Saddam Hussein has to understand the gravity of the situation.

No one wants war and globally everyone is in consent with this idea. However, the troops will go into Iraq, unfortunately, and fighting will start. It will not be a full blown war, as measures will be taken to stop it from continuing. Many people's lives are at stake. The innocent people are always victims in an ego battle. Unfortunately, the Iraqis are a poor people, with a weak economy and a very insecure lifestyle. Their constant fear of survival is devastating. No one should live in fear every minute of their lives.

Question: Mr. Bush made some valid points about Saddam's regime.

Answer: They were valid and extremely to the point. He was factual in his statements about the cruelty being imposed in Iraq. Yes, a better and more considerate leader would help Iraq from its tumultuous future. Saddam has to understand that he is facing a losing battle and his own life is at stake. His being ousted would be the best thing for the sanity of Iraq, for sure, child.

Question: Such tragedies are very hard to comprehend.

Answer: Well, child, these are consequences of egoistic leaders who fail to comprehend the reality of the situation. The greed and power that came with Saddam's position have left his intellect much to be desired. A peaceful resolution is not what he seeks, but revenge. His anger is out of proportion and it is only going to bring much heartache and suffering.

Thank you, Father.

Child, unfortunately this is the state of the world today. Bless you, child, go with peace and love. Remember ego and pride are destructive forces for mankind.

January 26, 2003

Question: Father, what is the meaning of having a pluralistic society?

Answer: In a pluralistic society, there are no distinctions between one's religion and belief. That is, all different people can live side by side with each other in harmony. There are no racial tensions or frustrations for each group of people and their religions.

Question: How do you think in today's climate, this can be achieved?

Answer: When all people realize and understand that each of us is God's creation, then and only then is this attainable. When there are class distinction, racial hatred and people differences, this cannot exist. I find it truly sad to see that people cannot accept each another as individuals. The hatred in some situations is so profound that it leads to killing another. These innocent victims are people either with a different ethnic background, skin coloring and have a high standing in society. The reasoning be-

Shahnaaz

hind this dislike is highly inhumane.

Education, child, does not give a person humility. It is the fact that they have to have the understanding and comprehension of compassion and love. Thinking only for the betterment of one's monetary status is not enough. Are material desires and needs the only true touchstones of one's life? Do these people contemplate these issues? Unfortunately they do not. Most of the current torment in today's worldly situation is due to this. If there are unrest and unease in one's own country, how can they expect to resolve the world's different issues?

Question: So it is like "charity begins at home?"

Answer: Yes, however it is not so easily done. No leader can change many individuals mind set of that country. No one changes anyone's attitude. One can try and show them the realities of the situation, but cannot physically change the biased mind.

It is a situation of total shame and loathing. Nonetheless, I pray that each individual has some form of enlightenment and brings about concern, care and love toward his brethren.

Thank you, Father. Go with wisdom, understanding, hope, love and care for all, child.

January 27, 2003

Question: Father, can you tell me about Imam Ali and his child-hood?

Answer: Child, I loved Ali. He was from the time of his birth, magnificent. He encompassed all the virtues of patience, toler-ance, kindness and courage. He was my most beloved of all. His compassion and care knew no bounds and he was always con-siderate of everyone around him. He was an absolutely loveable child, and had a really pleasant nature. He always smiled and brought a lot of peace to all around him. He was my favorite companion, son, brother and advisor. Our relationship was truly unique. As a child he loved to sit and listen to me for hours, he never troubled anyone and was always a pleasure to be with.

Question: He was always there for you in all the battles you fought.

Answer: Yes, most patiently and loyally. He never refused to help and protect me. He was simply amazing, child. His demean-or and strength were something to behold. He had learned to fight with his sword so eloquently that he could defend himself in any situation. People knew his art at swordsmanship and were scared of him. He was actually quite harmless. He never got angry and was always concerned about everyone around him.

Question: He must have been a wonderful son-in-law?

Answer: Fatima, could not have been more blessed. He was everything a wife would desire and a truly wonderful father as well.

Question: You must have been a proud grandfather?

Answer: Absolutely, child. They were my most precious children. I adored them immensely. Remember, child they were very special and gifted souls as well.

Question: What was your daughter, Bibi Fatima like in nature?

Answer: She was the encompassment of everything a good woman should be. She was a kind, considerate, intellectual, obedient child and a true ascetic. A great wife, daughter and mother. There was nothing lacking in Fatima. She was special, child.
Thank you, Father.

Child, I was truly blessed. I was lucky to have Fatima as a daughter, my grandson's Hassan and Hussein and most of all to have my beloved Ali, who I spent most of my life with. That alone to me was my greatest gift.

January 28, 2003

Question: Father, why did God create?

Answer: Child, God, in his mercy created everything in his desire so he could be able to feel and experience all of his creation. From the beginning of time, he knew that each creation would be interdependent on each other. This is the reason for the creating of different animals. All creation has a form of hierarchy, where the lowest is outdone by the highest. These were predetermined. What one sees as cruelty, is actually something preordained as survival. The most fit in any living hierarchy calls for this.

Question: Can you give me an example?

Answer: Well, let's look at mankind and its survival process. The more educated one is, the better its survival in the work force. The executives fare better than the blue collar worker. It is the same in the jungle.

Question: God surely knew that his creation would bring about ruin, cruelty and corruption on Earth?

Answer: God knows all, child. Yes he knew, but he again was hoping that his children would appreciate the environment they would live in. Their self-serving needs should not be blamed on him.

Understand, child, that his creation is not of this universe alone. His other creations have done remarkably well in other galaxies. His creation of mankind, has to him, in most cases been quite disappointing. He created purely and with clarity. He decided to give mankind free will and control of their destiny. He did not want to have a controlled environment where nothing would function independently. His mercy in giving man free will, only brought about misery to each other. That was of no fault of his, nor his desire.

God gives mercy to change situations and send us continuous guidance throughout the ages. Yet, mankind does not listen, again, to no fault of his own.

Question: It is difficult to see how animals consume each other for their own benefit?

Answer: Each living creation has a time span, and their survival is to consume that animal at a point in time. As said in the Quran, some creatures were made for the benefit of mankind as well as for consumption purposes.

Question: Are species in other Galaxies in a better situation?

Answer: Well, lets say Earth is in total decline. Most other species are usually quite united in their activities. Some do not have the need or feel the need to compete with each other, or the need for hatred amongst each other. The emotional insecurities and instabilities do not exist in these places. There are some species that are highly evolved both on a material or evolutionary stand, and as well as spiritually and scientifically as well. These creations do not need much help or guidance from God as they are able to work peacefully, independently and in an organized manner. They do not harm each another. So in fact, child, his creation in these areas have been quite beneficial.

Question: Do you feel mankind gives God grief?

Answer: Child, sincerely? Yes. We are God's most worrisome creation. He has had to send many different guides that have led distressed and sacrificial lives due to man's ego and greed. The tests of time, destiny and karma do not seem to be heeded by mankind. When one's ego and self-serving attitude takes over nothing is beneficial. Most assuredly, the outcome will be a grim if not chaotic one. However, all is not lost. We on the other side constantly seek for mankind's awareness to help themselves. It will take a long time, but change will come slowly. There is hope even in the Spiritual Realm.

Question: Besides the seven realms, are there any higher realms in the spiritual realm?

Answer: The seven spiritual realms are mortal realms. The eighth is an advanced realm of the Angelic Beings and the ninth is for Prophethood, and God sits or His Being is the supreme tenth realm.

Question: Have all Prophets reached the tenth realm?

Shahnaaz

Answer: Some have, child, others have not.

Question: You of course are at this point of total Nirvana?

Answer: Blessed I am, child, and being one with God is nothing short of ecstasy. That alone is not enough to describe the bliss.

Thank you, Father.
Child, I hope your quest for this knowledge has been met. Go with courage, wisdom, peace and understanding.

January 29, 2003

Conclusion

Question: Father, I am sure I can keep on asking myriad questions and you will always answer me quite lovingly. I hope that what I have asked is of vital importance. There are so many questions people would want and need to know. I honestly wish I could think of more. I wanted to ask questions that one would not be able to find in a library or while doing research on the internet. I wanted the conversations to be personal and of a sensitive nature in some cases. Once again, Father, I am very fortunate, blessed and privileged that you came to me. I am deeply grateful and thank you from the bottom of my heart for the courage you have given me to complete this book, which to me has been more than a "mission." Our conversations together have been most enlightening and knowledgeable. I hope the reader will gain insight into many areas of life as I have. I feel that I, and everyone who will read this book, is truly blessed to be able to find answers, with the help of our beloved Prophet Mohammed, to questions that have sought answers for centuries.

Shahnaaz

Answer: Child, daughter, I thank you for the time you took to compile this book of conversations between us. I hope it will enlighten many souls. My greatest task since I was on the Earth plane was to direct and instill the Truth, and to help bring about peace, harmony, love, respect, kindness and humanity to all on Earth. I tried to teach and set by example a life that would help bring about a more understanding and loveable society. I wanted equality amongst people, races and between man and woman. I wanted the children to be respected, despite the fact that they were either a girl or a boy. I did not want class or race distinctions, as all people are God's creatures. I desired for all God's children to love, care, have faith and trust in God. I am very sad to see how my teachings have been misinterpretated to benefit different leaders of some rigid Moslem thinkers. My children and people are viewed in a different light today in the world, because of a few false Moslems, who profess to be Moslems, but are nothing but evil doers. Islam is a religion that practices peace and love. I have never professed to take revenge, or have war on any person for whatever legitimate reason they may have. I have always maintained that any dissatisfaction can be resolved through peaceful measures and resolution. Power and ego struggles of leaders and so-called religious groups are not warranted. Many lives have been taken to prove a point, uselessly. Was it worth the effort, did it change the event or thinking? The world and its people have to come to a compromising situation.

Monetary and material greed makes the leaders of great nations lose the notion of humanity. Self-serving and self-gratification attitudes are the cause of great harm on a global level as well as on an individual one. The affliction of the poor, the distraught and the suffering are overlooked for the benefit of one's material well being. Are we not all created by God? Can we not understand and feel the plight of another? Are we so self engrossed in our own lives that we cannot see beyond our current situation?

All I ask and beseech to all the people is to understand the world as it is today. Why is there so much bloodshed, corruption and cruelty?

Why can we not come to a compromising solution? Man is only interested in his current surroundings, and tends to shut out anything else that is disturbing or troubling. Every single one of us can make a difference and can change the present Earthly situation. No child of God's should suffer without some hope or help from another of his fellow individuals.

Only our attitudes will make a difference for the future generations to come. Only we can make the future a better one, each of us. I love all my children, and I pray for each one constantly. It makes me very sad to see the destruction of my children and how they are wrongfully treated.

The effects of a few displaced individuals have made my children and Islam a target of mockery and shame. Islam is and was a religion of compassion and humanity. I am deeply troubled at how it is being portrayed in today's climate.

All children are God's children and I love all the people on the Earth plane. I pray for each of you. God bless each person. May God give everyone peace, harmony, compassion, understanding and most of all wisdom and the intellect to care for all.

Thank you again, Father, it has been truly a wonderful and inspiring journey.

Child, I love you. Go in peace, wisdom, understanding and God bless you always.